MW00914037

The Optimal Salesperson

Mastering the Mindset of Sales Superstars and Overachievers

Dan Caramanico & Marie Maguire

Foreword by David Kurlan, Author of Baseline Selling & CEO Objective Management Group, Inc.

www.optimalsaleperson.com

Library of Congress Control Number 2009934384
ISBN: 978-0-9802118-5-6

Books are available for special promotions and premiums. For
details, contact Special Markets, LINX, Corp., Box 613, Great
Falls, VA 22066, or e-mail specialmarkets@linxcorp.com.

Book design by Paul Fitzgerald
Editing by Sandra Gurvis

Published by LINX

LINX, Corp.
Box 613
Great Falls, VA 22066
www.linxcorp.com

Book website: www.optimalsaleperson.com

Printed in the United States of America

Dedication

Josephine, Betty, Daniel, Richard, Diana,
Geoff, Joanna and the many people who helped
us become who we are.

Acknowledgements

This book is based in large part on the lessons we learned in working with thousands of salespeople over more than two decades. We would like to acknowledge each of them for the contributions they made to our understanding of what makes up the optimal sales person.

However several of them stand out from the crowd either by the success they achieved, the help they gave us along the journey, or by what they were able to help us learn. Thus we would especially like to thank in alphabetical order Don Brown, Rush Burkhardt, Anthony Caraffa, Robert Cenci, Dan Citrenbaum, John DiBenedetto, Don DelMonte, Bill Finnegan, John Gualtieri, Terry Ives, David Kale, Dave Kurlan, Scott Lawhorne, Mark Lehman, Bill Loftus, Bill Messerschmidt, Kirk Miller, Chris Perks, Linda Resnick and John Rhoads.

We would also like to thank our executive assistant Heidi Binder for her tireless efforts in keeping us both on the straight and narrow over the last 13 years and Steve Eunpu our publisher who demystified the process of producing a book and paved the way toward publication.

CONTENTS

The Changing Face of Sales

Selling has undergone profound changes in recent years. Rather than using salespeople to learn about products and services, prospects can easily find whatever they need on the Internet. Transactional sales have also moved there, leaving eight basic categories that require the services of salespeople. These include:

1. Complex sales with a long sales cycle that require many visits and conversations

2. High-priced products or services, also with long sales cycles

3. The industry underdog who is not as well-known and must sell to overcome resistance

4. Design-built and custom-engineered products

5. Sales that require telling a story to make a product or service more desirable

6. Pioneers in a new technology, product, or service

7. No competition so buyers aren't looking for you or it

8. Lots of competition where sellers must differentiate and decommoditize themselves.

In addition to these categories, the economy adds a thick layer of resistance, providing salespeople with even more obstacles to success. Economic factors include:

- No money
- Spending freezes
- Not doing anything right now
- Cutting back
- Doing it ourselves
- Cancellations
- Delayed closings

A third dimension that further complicates selling today is choosing a selling methodology. In generic terms, approaches include:

- Customer-Focused Selling
- Relationship Selling
- Consultative Selling
- Transactional Selling
- Traditional Selling

Whether you are attempting to improve your sales ability, survive the recession, make more money, or manage salespeople more effectively, these options are so vast as to be almost overwhelming. Add the recent glut of sales books to the mix and it's simple to become confused: Which sales process? Which type of selling? What category am I in? What should I do differently? Which book?

Fortunately, Dan Caramanico and Marie Maguire have cut through the noise and provided a blueprint for success, a holistic, integrated, and complete sales career makeover. The authors describe what most salespeople do - on purpose, by accident, by purposeful accident – and why it does or doesn't work. And along with pointing out pitfalls, they tell you what it takes to become an Optimal Salesperson.

Dan and Marie also explain how to overcome some of the nastiest, most powerful, and most detrimental obstacles that salespeople face... their hidden weaknesses. As a reader, you may see yourself in the one or more of the examples provided in the book. You may discover, perhaps for the first time, why you haven't achieved the success you've been striving for. However, if you take their examples to heart, recognize your own weaknesses, and learn how to strengthen your focus, sales will become much simpler and easier.

If you're looking for straightforward, down-to-earth advice on how to become an Optimal Salesperson, the answers can be found right here, right now, in these pages.

David Kurlan
Author of Baseline Selling &
CEO Objective Management Group, Inc.

THE OPTIMAL SALESPERSON

How to Use This Book

This book will help you understand what constitutes an Optimal Salesperson. This information can be extremely useful in three ways: You might want to become an Optimal Salesperson, you may want to hire an Optimal Salesperson, or you may want to develop your current sales team into Optimal Salespeople.

THE OPTIMAL SALESPERSON is organized with these goals in mind. Part I is devoted to defining an Optimal Salesperson -- what they are, what they are not, and what they should be. You may recognize yourself or your colleagues in the examples in Chapter 1 – these are real people, although names and certain details have been changed to protect their privacy. Chapter 2 describes how these individuals developed to near-optimal status. Chapter 3 ties it all together by describing the essential attributes of the Optimal Salesperson. You may find yourself referring to Chapter 3 again and again.

Part II describes how the optimal sales person gets motivated and stays motivated on a day to day basis.

Part III describes the tools the optimal sales person must possess. A plan and a way to track progress, how to prospect in the most efficient manner, how to select a selling system that will be effective and suit your style and industry and the most important selling skills you must possess are all discussed in detail in chapters 6 through 9.

Part IV focuses on identifying and overcoming hidden obstacles such as the need for approval, money weaknesses, buying cycle, self-limiting beliefs, and more.

Part V takes the concept of hidden obstacles a step further by applying them to specific parts of the selling process from cold calling to referrals to pushing the edges of your comfort zone. Along with teaching you how to identify important traits in hiring an Optimal Salesperson.

Chapter 21 puts it all together, both in terms of achieving exponential growth and selling in a difficult and challenging economy.

This book represents the first step in your journey towards becoming an Optimal Salesperson and helping others reach their goals as well. We wish you luck, although you likely won't need it if you apply the principles it describes.

Dan Caramanico and Marie Maguire
Caramanico Maguire Associates, Inc.
www.caramanico.com

PART I

DEFINING THE OPTIMAL SALESPERSON

1

Who Are the Sub-Optimal Salespeople?

In defining an Optimal Salesperson, it's easier to begin by describing what he or she is <u>not</u>. Through the examples discussed in this chapter, you can begin to identify the common mistakes many salespeople make and begin to correct them in your own work or within your own team.

The following examples are based on real people. While the problems they face are described accurately, the product lines, genders and certain other details have been altered. As you read through the three examples, you may recognize yourself or others.

HARDWORKING HARRY

A strong work ethic made Harry the top salesperson in a company that sells high-end industrial systems valued at $250,000 and up. In a team of 18 salespeople doing just under $20 million per year, he consistently produced $2.5 million –

more than double the production of the average salesperson. Years of industry experience coupled with in-depth product knowledge gave him tremendous credibility with prospects. In addition, he was the epitome of professional; he dressed well, along with being articulate and respectful.

Harry had a great deal of expertise and technical knowledge; problem-solving was his strength. In his prior career as a design engineer he was accustomed to working long hours to meet deadlines. In fact whenever the client encountered any difficulty, Harry quickly leapt to the rescue.

As a result, clients loved him. Who wouldn't love a salesperson who gave so much free advice and solved so many problems with no pay? Harry just figured it was all part of the job.

But Harry spent very little time with his family. His kids complained that he missed their soccer games and his wife rarely saw him before 7:30 p.m. Management was happy with his production; however, both Harry and his supervisor were at a loss as to how he could meet the higher sales number that management was demanding for the next year. He simply could not work any harder. Harry put in ten hours a day, producing volumes of proposals with little or no help from the technical support team. He was constantly learning the nuances of a new product or spending time with prospects, whether they were qualified or not. He seemed the model salesperson, leading the team in numbers and outworking everyone in the building.

Yet when it came to actual selling, Harry fell short. No one had ever sat down with him and taught him how to sell effectively. Questions, when he asked them, were technical in nature and superficial. Harry never asked a tough question, one that would make the prospect feel uncomfortable in any way. He saw this as pressure; and pressuring a prospect in any way, Harry believed, showed a lack of respect and professionalism.

However, Harry often left a client's office confused about exactly what he should do next. When his manager debriefed him and asked pointed questions about the prospect's buying motivation, Harry's answers were usually vague. Although he was big on determining needs and collecting lots of data, on doing detailed analyses and responding with quotes, he was reluctant to discuss money.

So, whenever he prepared a quote he never knew what the prospect's budget was. His thinking was that it was none of his business. Similarly the prospect never had any idea what Harry's product was going to cost until the final proposal was in, resulting in major sticker shock. Consequently, Harry spent even more time revising proposals, negotiating price (usually down) and pleading with management to make concessions.

Harry's engaging personality and willingness to work hard won him business and kept clients coming back for more. He was good at following up and being persistent. However, Harry didn't actually focus on selling; and he was on the road to burning himself out by trying to please clients and placate management at the same time.

Harry lacked control of the selling process. Every opportunity was a new adventure and took a different, often unpredictable path. This drove his manager to distraction, since forecasting sales with Harry was like picking winning lottery numbers.

The same was true with quotes. Any time a prospect requested a quote, Harry launched into action, feverishly working to come up with the best design and the best (lowest) quote possible, calculated to three decimal places. But he failed to consider the opportunity's qualifications.

What if they couldn't afford his product? What if they had a bigger budget that allowed them to spend even more than the complete, accurate and detailed quote that he believed set him apart from the competition?

As a result of his inability to control the selling process, Harry wasted a lot of time with unqualified prospects and his close rate was low, despite his hard, incessant work.

UNDERPERFORMING URSULA

Ursula's go-to-market strategy consisted of exceptional service and expansive industry knowledge. She assumed that her twenty years of experience would be the main reason people hired her to help them profit from their real estate investments. She focused on her clients and their needs and had a natural bent toward over servicing.

However, when it came to actual selling, she tended to shut down, adjusting her service offerings on a regular basis. Her sales calls were usually an information dump as she tried to impress the client with her wealth of knowledge. She spent most of her time in front of the prospect expounding on her experience or trying to solve their problems in an attempt to win them over. Often by the time the sales call was over, the prospect had all the information he or she needed.

Ursula's sales process was simple -- bid, bid, bid, and hope. She'd honed her pitch to perfection. Her belief was that if she just could get the prospect to listen, they would understand how valuable her services were. She couldn't understand why they weren't buying since they seemed so positive during the first meeting. Second meetings were often cancelled if she managed to set one up at all. As coordinated as her sales pitch was, when the prospect asked questions it got her off track.

She tried to answer as completely as she could while giving as much information as possible. She pitched her service passionately and, when the prospect engaged with her, she "winged it" all the way to the close. Her strongest sales asset was her absolute conviction that she could help the prospect increase revenue.

Ursula possessed some excellent selling abilities, such as bonding with prospects quickly and developing rapport with virtually anyone. However, the thought of making a cold call was enough to induce a stress attack. And she needed to strengthen her questioning skills and work on how to effectively handle objections. In addition, she was confused about how and exactly when to close a sale.

When she changed jobs and moved to the financial industry, her conviction coupled with her sincere desire to help got her off to a quick start. However, when the economy started to bottom out, she ran into trouble and allowed her emotions to get in the way. And other external factors, such as the outcome of her most recent sale, also affected her attitude. A sale meant her ship had finally come in but if she lost a deal or two she became convinced she would never get another sale. She could be positive and enthusiastic one day and overly negative about her future the next.

However, a few months after her switch to the financial industry, her sales began to improve. She consistently employed an effective selling process, but her emotions were still out of control. Her income had increased and her bills were getting paid regularly, but she was still not earning enough to achieve her personal goals. By some measures she was successful but she constantly struggled to stay on an even keel. The emotional energy she expended in executing her new selling skills and struggling to break out of her comfort zone took a tremendous toll. She was getting by but wasn't enjoying her work.

Despite her progress, Ursula was still stalled at a relatively low production level. Part of this was due to the fact that she came from a relatively poor background and had low expectations of herself. As a result of her fear of success and breaking out her comfort zone, she resigned herself to the "fact" that she would never achieve a higher income bracket. Every time she got to a new level, she stayed there only briefly before dropping back to one she felt comfortable with. Management, however, was happy with her average production. They saw potential for bigger and better things but were content with what she gave them. Still, Ursula wanted more.

STUCK STEVE

Passion for his craft set Steve apart. He was an architect and very proud of it. His father had been an artist and passed along to his son a love of the aesthetic and the talent to turn people's dreams into reality. He had been in private practice for a number of years but was struggling mightily.

Any rational analysis of Steve's situation would indicate that he should give up his practice and go to work for someone else. But he soldiered on. He didn't really feel that he had any other option. He had sunk everything he owned into the business, was in a lot of debt, and would never dig himself out if he didn't turn a profit.

In his efforts to improve, Steve turned into a student of sales. He took copious notes in class and attended every seminar. In-class exercises were always a snap. He always knew which technique to use in which situation. He was the ideal student; attentive in class, asking good questions, and always willing to share his thoughts and experiences.

But Steve was unable to put his knowledge into practice. Although he was articulate and said the "right" things, he had a very low self-concept and little tolerance for risk. Consequently he always took the safe route. He never challenged a prospect or asked a tough question and always tried to hang in with every prospect as long as possible.

Steve did internalize certain aspects of selling. He had a plan and worked it diligently. He had a well-defined sales process that he followed regularly. He always attempted to ask questions and qualify his prospect but his efforts were usually thwarted. Since he primarily engaged selling at an intellectual level, he focused his attention on steps in the sales process and the nuances of executing sales techniques. When he failed, he could always find the reason in some misapplication of the techniques. Although his self-limiting belief systems were pointed out to him and discussed at great length in the classes he attended, he refused to alter them, even though he knew that change could have a dramatic effect on his income. He just worked harder at the "tangible" aspects of selling – a different way to turn a phrase, a new approach in discussing money, an exciting method to get the prospect thinking about return on investment, and innovative and different ways of prospecting.

Fear had him stymied; fear of losing what he had, fear of losing a deal because he was too aggressive, fear of being rejected, and fear of getting a "no." Yet he failed to consider the fact that he might be losing both the respect of his peers because of his unwillingness to change and income by letting sales slip through his fingers. Nor did he seem concerned about disappointing his family because he could barely give them the basics, not to mention mounting debt.

Steve was afraid to take any risks on a sales call. He had to be 100 percent sure that what he said would be well-received and pose little chance of recrimination by the prospect before he would try anything new. He worried that the prospect would not like him and that asking a tough question would somehow detract from the message he was trying to deliver. He was overly worried about his reputation in the industry. He could not see that being a doormat did little to enhance his status.

Steve also had issues with money concepts. Relatively small sums seemed like a king's ransom and when a deal seemed large he got excited. Once that occurred the prospect had total control and could easily maneuver him away from the selling process. The bigger the deal, the more he was willing to abandon his sales posture and do whatever the prospect asked.

Steve was stuck on a treadmill. His primary goal was to get out of debt. His other goals, a bigger house and college tuition for his kids, were admirable, but deep down inside Steve did not believe that he could achieve them. Nor did he really believe in himself; he was working hard without knowing exactly what he was trying to accomplish and without any real sense of purpose.

2

From Sub-Optimal to Optimal

Harry, Ursula, and Steve were motivated to improve and grow as salespeople. Harry and Ursula got very close to optimal while Steve hit a plateau.

HARDWORKING HARRY: HARDLY WORKING

Revenue Quadruples

Competition for major orders is something Harry rarely sees anymore. His prospecting consistently uncovers potential deals in their formative stage. He is able to shape them early, gain the client's confidence, get them to take the project "off the street," and negotiate a contract that is fair to both parties. His sales now exceed $10 million per annum; quadruple what they had been only three years ago. His forecasts are extremely accurate, which makes management's job much easier. If Harry says that a project will hit in the second quarter, it will. He wins without competition, which is the essence of selling at its finest. When Harry prepares a quote, he knows in advance whether it is budgetary, designed to keep a competitor honest, or a written in such a way that will lead to an order.

He frequently works through engineers who specify and procure his product on behalf of the end user. They tell him when the procurement is meant for him and when he should not bother because another company's product is superior for that particular application. He also mostly talks with decision-makers who treat him like a trusted advisor and not a vendor. The new Harry is easy to manage, the company is more profitable, he is making more money, and his family sees him for dinner every night.

More Comfortable at Higher Levels

Harry's comfort zone has changed dramatically. In the past, he'd been thrilled to exceed $2 million in sales per year, now he feels like he is underperforming if he is not averaging $2 million per quarter. Big is now small for Harry. Large projects for him used to be in the $250,000 range. Now he considers a $600,000 project a small one.

Obviously this means he needs fewer projects to meet his numbers. He can be more selective and only pursue contracts with a high probability of winning. No more bidding and hoping for wins. His margins are also higher since the client sees value in what Harry and his company provide. Because he works on larger projects, he interacts at the executive level in the client organization. He is now comfortable in that atmosphere and avoids getting bogged down in needless detail. They welcome his tough questions and customer-centric method of selling. They provide him the information he needs to give his product a competitive advantage. By the time the competition finds out about a project, Harry is usually the virtual incumbent.

Effective and Efficient Selling Skills

Harry now qualifies the prospect relentlessly, something he rarely did in the past. He realizes that the prospect has to qualify in order for him to spend time with them, instead of the other way around. He always quantifies the amount of money the problem is costing the client and ascertains how much they are willing to spend to fix it.

Rather than focusing on his product when talking with a client, Harry also now focuses on the client and their problems. He has conversations with clients; he does not sell to them. Once he has the client engaged, he skillfully leads the conversation while letting the prospect do most of the talking. The focus is on the prospect, the problem at hand, and its ramifications throughout the organization.

By the time the first meeting is over, he has a complete understanding of the organization and how the project will progress through the client's procurement process. He finds someone in the organization who can serve as his internal champion; this individual can introduce him to those with an interest in the project who can influence its outcome.

Harry has a clear idea of what the next step is, so every meeting ends with a plan of action. If the project stalls because its urgency disappears, the money dries up, or his product ceases to be the leading solution, Harry ends the pursuit gracefully and moves on to more fertile ground.

Questions are his stock in trade. He is able to anticipate prospects' difficulties by asking tough, thought-provoking questions. In this manner, the prospect can acknowledge the issue or redirect him to the actual problem area. When he receives conflicting information from the client, he confronts them calmly and professionally to get the situation cleared up. They appreciate Harry's ability to get the heart of the matter quickly.

Harry responded to the downturn in the economy by increasing his sales activity. This way he was able to grow his pipeline in anticipation of deals being put off to some future date or cancelled. Since he is proactive and modifies his behavior to meet changing market conditions he is still able to make his numbers every quarter.

Hardly Working, but Still Needs Some Work

Sixty-five hour work weeks are now a thing of the past. He has challenges, but is in control of his workload. Support staff don't mind working on his proposals since they almost always result in a sale. There is little to no wasted energy on Harry's part since he has control of the selling process and it's no longer a mystery to him. He is not only stress-free; he recently confessed to us that at times he is actually bored.

Harry's productivity has increased eightfold, quadrupling sales while halving hours worked. He no longer wastes time on fruitless proposals. Plus he no longer has to expend a vast amount of emotional and mental energy on the selling process, instead using it in ways that will benefit his family and personal life. Management leaves him alone, preferring to spend their time on the non-producers. Harry is very close to being the Optimal Salesperson, but still needs work in certain areas.

While Harry was emotionally prepared for sales, he needed a better selling process and improved selling skills. His ability to understand his problem areas helped him make a dramatic improvement in a relatively short time. However, he still needs to work on planning. He sets and commits to aggressive goals, but still refuses to create a sales plan as to how he is going to get there. He feels it is a waste of time to determine his closing rate, his average sale, and how much selling activity -- meetings, calls, and so on -- it takes to close the average deal. The only number he tracks is the bottom line, meaning the number of sales he makes and the revenue he brings in. As a result of not knowing what he did to get to this level it will be hard to figure out how to get out of a slump. It will also be difficult to determine just what he has to do to get to the next level, even though he's doing extremely well right now and is content. And, at the moment, management is happy with him as well.

UNDERPERFORMING URSULA: UP, UP AND AWAY

Top Two Percent Performer

Calm, cool, and collected is how most of Ursula's colleagues describe her these days. In the midst of a downturn in the housing market and turmoil in the financial markets she is breaking sales records. Twelve million was her peak month and she routinely averages $6 million per month, about four times what the average person in her profession produces.

Part of one of the largest financial institutions in the country, Ursula has received a high level of recognition. When the president of the company comes to town he stops in to see her; she has also been named one of the top 30 out of the company's 1400 salespeople.

Like Harry, Ursula's success came with far less effort than she was expending when she was getting only average results. Ursula has built a support team around her that allows her to only focus on the important aspects of selling. Even more amazing is that she was able to start a new venture in which she earned $400,000 over a three-year period while dramatically increasing her production in her primary job as a financial salesperson. Obviously she has gotten very efficient!

It's All about Expectation and Process

Ursula had a difficult time accepting her success. At first she attributed it to the market or luck and thought it couldn't last. Eventually, she had to accept the fact that she was good at what she did and that she deserved the rewards she received. Finally she got over the last hurdle which was to own the responsibility for her success. She now truly believes that she belongs in the rarefied atmosphere in which she finds herself. She needed to learn how to become comfortable at the higher levels. Once that happened, she no longer felt like a trespasser at the corporate awards ceremony. She stopped wasting energy worrying about whether she belonged and stopped panicking when she had a bad week. She was then able to focus on getting referrals, meeting people, and solving their financial problems. She could finally enjoy her success and relax with it, which in turn brought even more success.

Expectation is the key to Ursula's success. She anticipates big numbers, so when she has a big month it does not unnerve her as it had in the past. When Ursula gets in front of a prospect she expects them to open up and share their problems with her, so they do. When Ursula can help with the problem she expects the prospect to choose her even though she rarely has the lowest price in the industry. She expects her clients to give her referrals, so they do. She never communicates this expectation verbally, but the people she deals with sense her confidence and react accordingly.

Ursula now has a very effective sales process that she has internalized. She does not consciously go from Step 1 to Step 2 but touches all of the bases in a logical order for a particular situation. As a result of this, prospects rarely if ever feel sold. They feel like they are in control and are calling the shots. Ursula is just there to help. Sales techniques are not a major part of her selling. Whereas she used to consciously try to execute techniques she learned, now she just converses with the prospect and moves them through the process seamlessly. She jokingly refers to her style as the non-technique technique.

As the Optimal Salesperson, Ursula produces amazing results with little effort. Management and her prospects love her and she is meeting all of her personal goals. Best of all, she enjoys her work and is happy.

STUCK STEVE-STILL STUCK

Stuck Steve remains frustrated and has been at the same level for over five years. The economy has a major effect on his production. When the economy is hot his sales are up. When the economy turns down his sales suffer in greater proportion than others. He still gets excited over relatively small projects and remains intimidated by large ones. And he's still a prisoner of his fear, refusing to take emotional risks in interactions with prospects. He continues to seek approval from everyone he interacts with. Because of these factors, his real goals remain uncertain and unmotivating. Consequently he is still right where he was...emotionally comfortable, financially strapped, and totally frustrated. He is not making enough to get ahead and owes too much to quit.

Steve is now an expert in what "should" be done on sales calls. Intellectually he knows more about selling than many people making double or triple his salary. Yet Steve has failed to internalize the process.

Although Steve gives sales plenty of effort, he needs to redirect his energies. Instead of working hard at learning and doing, he should be taking measured risks and dealing with the emotional consequences. The struggle for success is not between Steve and his prospect; it is within Steve himself. He must recognize that the problem lies in his fear of failure and need for approval. Even though he is scared, he needs to understand that he must take a chance in executing the techniques he instinctively knows are right, although they may involve risk. He must step out of his comfort zone regularly and understand that indeed risk can involve failure but sometimes you must fail in order to succeed. And if you do fail, then you can try again.

By accepting the possibility of failure, he can face his fears and realize that most are unfounded. And even if he does get rejected or speak out of turn, the consequences won't be as dire as he might project in his mind. Paradoxically, the more he fails the braver he will become because the risk is reduced – after all, what he feared didn't happen. The braver he gets the better questions he will ask, the more qualified his prospects will be, and the higher his close rate will go. His confidence will increase, his comfort zone will be raised, and he will become braver still. The cycle will repeat itself over and over like it has for others who have made it to the top of the sales profession. Steve needs to step up his game and be willing to take risks as well as ownership for his lack of results.

HOW DID THEY DO IT?

As you can see, Harry and Ursula worked hard to become Optimal Salespeople. It took an intense desire to succeed, an unwavering commitment to face internal obstacles, and emotional energy applied in the right places to accomplish their transformation. The length of the journey will vary with the individual but anyone can achieve success in sales if they are willing to put in the time and energy. Steve is still struggling, but with more effort and emotional conviction he can become an Optimal Salesperson as well.

They Took Responsibility

Many salespeople refuse to take responsibility, coming up with a variety of excuses. "The economy is bad," "Our prices are too high," and "Prospects don't get it" are just some of the many rationalizations. What Harry, Ursula and even Steve did was step back, take an objective look at the situation and decide that, regardless of what was going on around them, it was up to them to adjust and succeed anyway. After careful analysis – and with some outside help -- they were able to recognize what they were doing that was contributing to their unacceptable results.

Once they recognized the problem (again with some help), they took decisive action <u>by changing their actions.</u> They revised their approach to the customers. They modified their sales process to a more effective one. They improved their method of questioning and acquired new skills to help deal with negative selling situations that seemed to form a pattern. Most importantly however, they looked inward to discover what was getting in their way during sales calls. What were they thinking and feeling? Parts IV and V will discuss what we call <u>hidden obstacles.</u> Luckily Harry didn't have too many. Ursula had plenty but overcame most of them and Steve is still a work in progress.

They Took Risks

Taking risk is something businesspeople do every day. It is usually an intellectual process, weighing expected gains and costs with an estimated return on investment appropriate to the level of risk. Sometimes gains and costs are monetary and sometimes not, but they are almost always intellectual in nature. However, these are not the type of risks Harry, Ursula and Steve took. They were asked to take <u>emotional risks.</u> This is the risk you take when you are uncomfortable asking for a referral but you do it anyway. You are putting yourself in a position to be rejected. It is also emotionally risky to be afraid to call at the top of an organization; or to try a new sales technique for the first time; or make a major alteration to your sales process by changing the order in which you do things. All of these activities are easy for some people and difficult for others. It all depends on the hidden weaknesses you bring to the job. Taking risk requires emotional energy, as anyone who has made their first walk-in cold call can attest. Lots of risk-taking and hence emotional energy is required before you can achieve dramatic growth.

They Got Help

While not absolutely necessary, mentors can be a tremendous help in achieving success. Someone who has already been down the jungle trail can point out where the trip wires are. Objective observation of your actions and results will help you adjust your sales activities appropriately. While some people are capable of self-analysis, most are not. So it's in your best interest to find someone who has succeeded in sales and ask them to mentor you. It can be a co-worker, a sales manager, someone from another company or even a professional sales trainer or coach. Harry, Ursula and Steve took the latter approach and hired us to help them. Having been through the process ourselves, we could analyze what was holding them back and came equipped with processes and techniques that could guide them to overcoming the barriers they faced. We could adapt what we knew to their particular situation - as anyone who mentors you should adapt what they know to your world. There are no "one size fits all" systems out there.

Although it is the manager's job to mentor and grow salespeople, the real world is often quite different. Many sales managers lack the knowledge and discipline to help their sales force grow and, in this increasingly lean economy, many salespeople do not have full-time sales managers.

So how did Harry, Ursula, and to a limited extent, Steve do it? Chapter 3 will explain how the various pieces fit together, and what makes up the Optimal Salesperson.

THE OPTIMAL SALESPERSON

3

Essential Attributes of the Optimal Salesperson

What attributes actually determine who will be successful in sales? Is it a winning personality, technical knowledge, or an amiable social style? Or is it something as obtuse as wearing a certain color or item of jewelry? Consider, for example, athletes and their fans. Whenever Bob watches his favorite baseball team on TV they always seem to win but when he listens on the radio they lose. In mathematical terms, there seems to be a correlation between how he views the game and its result. Is it reasonable to assume that Bob is causing the outcome? To draw that conclusion would be ridiculous. This is a pure case of correlation without causality.

However, Bob's favorite player Bill notices that sometimes he hits better when he wears his left sock inside out. This is true about 65 percent of the time. Is it reasonable to assume that the state of Bill's sock is causing his success? Probably not, but deeper study might reveal that when it's inside out Bill feels more confident. Confidence allows him to concentrate more and hence have better results. However, correlation data alone could mislead observers into looking at the status of players' socks to make in-game decisions.

It turns out that when Bill is confident of success he is successful 95 percent of the time regardless of the condition of his sock. The sock generally gives him confidence but sometimes he looks up and sees a 6'10" pitcher getting ready to throw the ball 98 miles per hour six inches from his belt buckle and he gets intimidated. Confidence against the pitcher then might be deemed to be an essential attribute of success in hitting a baseball. A manager trying to decide whether or not to let Bill bat in a particular situation would be better served to gauge his confidence against that pitcher than to make his decision based on the condition of his left sock.

CORRELATIONS TO SUCCESS

The essential attributes listed in this chapter have a causal relationship to success in sales. Testing of over 400,000 salespeople during the last 20 years by the Objective Management Group, Inc. has proven that there is a very high correlation between the factors listed in Figure 1-1 and success in sales.

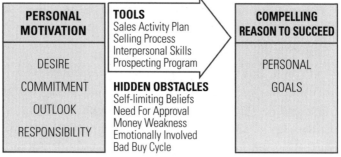

THE OPTIMAL SALESPERSON

Figure 1.1. Factors for Success in Sales

Figure 1.1 represents the relationship among the essential attributes of the Optimal Salesperson. A general overview of these attributes will be discussed in this chapter; succeeding chapters will delve into more detail.

A COMPELLING REASON TO SUCCEED

All motivation for salespeople is self-motivation. Salespeople will do more to meet the goals they set for themselves than to meet a corporate goal handed down to them. More than any other person in their company, salespeople need a constant and compelling <u>reason to succeed</u>.

Everyone in the organization has obstacles in doing their jobs. However, salespeople face especially daunting tasks. They not only have to fight demons within themselves in the form of fear of rejection, need for approval, and other emotional factors, but they have people who are actively trying to impede them from reaching their goals. Gatekeepers try to prevent them from seeing prospects. Competitors try to undercut their price and "steal" business from them. Even prospects are often not generally cooperative, asking hard questions and trying to get more for their money.

Unlike other kinds of jobs, salespeople just cannot just "show up" for work and clock out at the end of the day. Optimal Salespeople need a vision to remind them of why they are doing battle every day. Without daily encouragement, they tend to remain in their comfort zone, stunting their own growth and that of the company.

A <u>vision</u> is a clear picture of what your personal future will look like. To be effective, the vision should begin with a 5-10 year look ahead. Then it should be broken into yearly, quarterly, weekly and even daily milestone goals. Chapter 4 is devoted on helping you establish and measure progress toward the vision.

PERSONAL MOTIVATION

Developing a clear vision and putting goals in writing are only the first steps. You must have motivation to accomplish the sales activity and achieve the goals.

Desire

Desire is the drive to acquire or accomplish something. The single most important attribute in a salesperson, desire cannot be forced upon a person or taught in class. In sales, desire is usually the drive to sell products or services so that things can be acquired with the commission earned by doing so.

A salesperson requires more desire than other types of jobs. Engineers, clerks, accountants, laborers, and others can arrive at work, deal with whatever comes their way, and then go home, often without feeling as if they've made a tremendous emotional investment. While desire is needed to excel in production and management, it takes about 10 times more desire to excel in sales as the authors, who have worked in both sales and delivery, can attest. Relatively few engineers and managers have failed due to lack of desire. However, many seemingly talented salespeople lacked the desire to push through the internal and external barriers necessary for success in the sales arena. Chapter 5 has more details on desire and becoming an Optimal Salesperson.

Commitment

Commitment is the measure of what you will give up to achieve a goal. Commitment and desire are opposite sides of the motivation coin. They are both crucial and, like desire, commitment cannot be taught and must be innate.

Desire without commitment is just wishful thinking. Imagine the salesperson who has a compelling reason to succeed and has intense desire to get there (or so they say) but lacks commitment. This person will wilt at the first sign of personal risk or resistance from a prospect. They might think to themselves: "I really want to double my income … Oh, you want me to make a cold call?" "Do I have to ask that question? … Actually I'm afraid to do that right now…" Without commitment they will remain at the status quo, neither increasing their revenue nor their knowledge. Although we see plenty of people with desire and no commitment we can't remember ever seeing a person with commitment and no desire. After all, who would commit to making 30 cold calls a day without a desire to sell something? Chapter 5 will elaborate more on commitment.

Outlook

Attitude about the state of the world and life in general can magnify or miniaturize the effect of desire and commitment. A person's attitude about the way things are in their world is considered to be their <u>outlook</u>. Your outlook can be optimistic -- you can think all things are possible -- or pessimistic; you believe nothing is possible. Or it can be somewhere in-between, as is often the case.

Outlook acts somewhat like a telescope. If viewed through the telescope the way it is designed, your goals and vision look near. They appear to be within easy reach and you can attack your selling tasks enthusiastically knowing you are so close. This is how a positive outlook works. However, if you peer through the wrong end of the telescope the goals appear much farther away than they actually are. The effect of a negative outlook on life is that you decide that "there is no use in doing anything today because these goals are so far away and the economy is so bad (or our prices are so high, or competition is so fierce, etc.) that I will never get there." A negative outlook undermines motivation. Obviously the Optimal Salesperson has a positive outlook most of the time. Chapter 5 will explain the effects of outlook in further detail.

Responsibility

An Optimal Salesperson never makes excuses. Excuses only diminish personal motivation to succeed. Some popular excuses that salespeople use to explain away their poor performance are the economy (no one is buying anything), product pricing (ours is too high), competition (there's too much), technical support (not enough or not good enough), marketing support (brochures are outdated, no good leads), and so on.

Excuse-making, the art of not taking responsibility for lack of results, is a deterrent to growth. If, for example, you tell yourself that the economy is bad or the company's prices are too high, that you get no support or the competition is undercutting you, then you don't really have to change You just have to wait until the world changes, then your sales will increase. You may think, "It's not my fault sales are down... so are everyone else's!"

But excuses lead to being resigned to the status quo. They affect not only your own outlook but the outlook of those around you and can result in a self-fulfilling prophecy and failure. Desire and commitment wane and the motivation to fight through obstacles, improve oneself, and meet goals disappears.

Optimal Salespeople take <u>personal responsibility</u> for lack of results no matter what. They understand that if they adjust their approach, tweak their selling process, increase sales activity, apply their selling skills, or change their beliefs they can increase their effectiveness, regardless of external circumstances. They also realize that an added benefit of taking responsibility and acting accordingly is that, when the economy does improve, pricing is more favorable or competition lessens, they will be in a much stronger position than the competition. They will probably also have a larger market share and higher margins.

TOOLS TO ACHIEVE SUCCESS

Everyone needs certain tools to be successful in their job, and the Optimal Salesperson is no exception. They include a sales activity plan, a prospecting program, an effective sales process, and interpersonal skills.

A Sales Activity Plan

<u>Sales activity</u> is a critical and irreplaceable element of success. How much activity is necessary varies and is a function of such things as the sales goal, the closing rate, the value of average sales, and so on.

Activities that lead directly to sales include the number of conversations and face-to-face meetings with decision-makers, the number of proposals, and even the number of times the salesperson picks up the phone and dials. Although other activities such as organizing prospect files, doing research, and learning the product are important, they don't lead directly to sales. The Optimal Salesperson ensures that selling activity -- the activity for which he or she gets paid -- gets done first. They establish activity goals for each day, week, and month and they also track their daily activity to ensure they are making adequate progress toward specific milestones.

Interestingly, critical activities rarely present themselves as urgent. It is never a crisis to make a sales call. Have you ever gotten a call that sounds like, "Mary, I was on your list to cold call today … you didn't call and I am upset!!" Or, "Randy, how long have I been your client … three years … have you ever one time asked me for a referral … What am I … a second class client?" However, many other sales tasks do show up as urgent. Management needs an updated forecast by the end of the day. Proposals need to go out this week. Marketing needs input. The desk is piled high with "to do's" which demand your immediate attention.

Regardless of these other tasks, the Optimal Salesperson tracks the amount of critical sales activity he or she does daily to make sure that the pipeline stays full with qualified prospects. They also fit so-called urgent activities in and around the most critical one of actually selling. Chapter 6 will discuss the importance of a sales activity plan and how to use it.

A Prospecting Program

Continuous <u>prospecting</u> is the lifeblood of a successful salesperson. What good is it to be an excellent closer if there are no prospects to talk to? And not just any prospect: the Optimal Salesperson knows what the ideal prospect looks like, how to make contact, and has a process for generating a steady stream of ideal prospects. Some may accomplish this by cold calling, some are networking junkies, and some have a pipeline that supplies them with a constant flow of referrals.

Optimal Salespeople also know which prospects are undesirable – the ones who are not profitable, too small, too big, or too much trouble and deter them from achieving their personal goals. Chapter 7 will explore prospecting in depth and will provide you with a process for generating a steady flow of introductions to the right prospects.

An Effective Sales Process

Consistent results are the hallmark of an <u>effective selling process</u>, which is basically a sequence of steps that you take a prospect through as you go from introduction to new customer. Rather than a brick wall which starts from the foundation up, a sales process is more like a series of gates or milestones that you must pass through as you move from beginning to end. The order may not matter – and in fact may vary from one individual to the next – but all milestones must be achieved and steps taken to achieve a successful result. The sales process serves as a guide as the sale progresses, a yardstick to help with prioritizing, and a standard to measure success.

However, few salespeople actually follow a sales process. But without a defined sales process, you'll find it difficult to control either individual sales meetings or the sales process as a whole. Prospects may take over the sale, causing salespeople to respond only to learn there's no money or that the decision has already been made to go with someone else. Many salespeople have no idea why they lost a project or, almost as bad, why they won.

The Optimal Salesperson is flexible in his or her approach and treats each opportunity as an individual event. But the flexibility occurs within the prescribed bounds of a well-defined process. For example, they would never prepare a quote for a prospect who didn't meet their qualifying criteria. Having specific criteria is all part of having a sales process.

There are many sales processes to choose from and depending on the circumstances, some are more effective than others. Chapter 8 will give you criteria to evaluate and choose those that are right for you and your particular situation.

Interpersonal Skills

Sales techniques are not as important to success as everyone thinks. Everyone wants to know the latest closing techniques or effective cold calling scripts. But belief systems are more important.

However, <u>interpersonal skills</u>, abilities which some people possess naturally and others need to develop through study and practice, are often overemphasized as criteria for being in sales. How often have you heard (or said) that, "Joe gets along well with people, let's put him in the sales department." (Incidentally, that is how both of the authors got their start in sales.) Skills alone do not make a sale. For example the ability to ask good questions is a good skill to have and will make a salesperson more effective to an extent. But the ability to ask good questions in the absence of an effective selling process will lead to only marginally better overall results because the questions may not lead the prospect to the close but rather down a wrong trail.

The Optimal Salesperson possesses good interpersonal skills but keeps them in their proper perspective. Like an effective mechanic with a garage full of tools, he or she picks just the right one for the particular job, understanding that is not about the "tools" but about making the sale.

Used correctly, interpersonal skills can translate into many abilities: to quickly establish a bond with a prospect, to close, to qualify a prospect, to get referrals, to ask tough questions when the situation calls for it, to call at the top, among others. Chapter 9 will delve into more detail.

THE HIDDEN OBSTACLES TO SUCCESS

Certain obstacles to success are obvious and can easily be remedied. This includes lack of product knowledge, time management problems and certain selling skills. Other obstacles to success are more subtle or <u>hidden</u> and not immediately obvious when you look at or interview a salesperson. These hidden obstacles have the biggest impact on success and cannot be found by reading a resume or even talking to a former employer. They are, generally speaking, emotional in nature and rooted in an individual's upbringing as well as his or her personal and professional history. It doesn't matter how or why the weaknesses were acquired but what they are, whether they exist, and how they can be overcome.

Self-limiting Beliefs

<u>Beliefs</u> are firmly held convictions about the way things are. It doesn't matter whether it is actually (objectively) true because for you there is no doubt. You know it is true because your experience tells you so. There's no room for discussion and those with differing opinions are obviously mistaken.

Like everyone else, salespeople have a number of self-limiting beliefs, but unlike others, these ideas can have a bigger effect on their results than sales techniques or even their sales process. For example, say Larry believes that people always buy based on price. He knows it's true because every prospect he comes in contact with seems to make price point the basis of their buying decisions. If you try to convince him otherwise, his many examples will refute your argument.

So we put him in a sales class for two days and teach him five time-tested, proven techniques to sell value over price. He has these down cold and executes the moves flawlessly. However, we do not attempt to change his belief about how prospects buy. On the third day Larry gets in front of a prospect and asks how the buying decision will be made. The prospect replies, "We are going to go with the lowest price." What happens to the techniques we taught Larry? That's right! They go right out the window! He thinks, "Makes sense, that's what I would do!" His newly acquired techniques remain unused and he has yet another data point to reinforce his self-limiting belief. Chapter 10 will get much deeper into this aspect of selling and how it can be overcome

Need For Approval

Excessive <u>need for approval</u> means that it is more important that the prospect "likes" the salesperson than actually do business with them. Naturally, it affects many areas of sales. Having too much need for the prospects' approval means that the salesperson will fail to execute a technique or step in a sales process that he or she perceives as too aggressive.

Which techniques do salespeople perceive to be aggressive? The ones that violate their belief systems, including the previously mentioned self-limiting beliefs. How and when need for approval affects salespeople depends on their beliefs and other hidden weaknesses. For example, if Mary thinks that requesting a referral is inappropriate before a project has been completed successfully, then any attempt to have her ask ahead of time will be perceived as an aggressive technique. This perception in combination with excessive need for approval will effectively limit the number of referrals Mary will get.

Can you imagine the effect if Mary believed that it was never appropriate to ask for the referral? It has happened, and even at the senior level. Mary and others like her can be high producers but work much too hard for the business they get. They do get referred from time to time but never ask for a referral, which if done on a regular basis, can completely eliminate all cold prospecting. The need for approval can magnify the effect of most other shortcomings and will be discussed in Chapter 11.

Uncontrolled Emotions

Being "in the moment" is essential to the ability of a salesperson to hear precisely not only what the prospect is saying but also appreciate the nuances and understand their ramifications. Getting at what the prospect is really trying to communicate is essential to the salesperson's ability to react appropriately.

Unfortunately, many salespeople miss hidden cues because they are not really listening. They fail to hear significant (as opposed to long) portions of a conversation because they were either thinking about what they were going to say next or silently talking to themselves.

This type of inward focusing is common behavior; however it can be especially devastating to a salesperson.

<u>Uncontrolled emotions</u> can happen when the prospect says or does something unexpected. The salesperson starts to think "How did this happen?" or "Now what should I do?" What they are NOT doing is paying attention to the prospect. They have "checked out" of the conversation for a few seconds. It is not unusual to check out for several 5-10 second intervals over a 2-5 minute stretch of conversation. If this happens during a critical point, the results can be devastating: missed cues, lost opportunities, shortened conversations, and lost sales.

When something unexpected occurs, the Optimal Salesperson reins in his or her immediate reaction, staying in the moment by asking a question, making a statement or otherwise skillfully redirecting the conversation. This can only happen when the salesperson remains detached and in control of their emotions. Chapter 13 will discuss this in more detail.

Money Weakness

Reluctance to talk about <u>money</u> is the most common hidden weakness and occurs in 65 percent of all salespeople. It's easy to understand why. Imagine you are nine years old at Thanksgiving dinner and turn to your Uncle Pat and ask, "How much money did you make last year?" What reaction would you have gotten?

At the very least you would have on the spot "coaching" about the inappropriateness of discussing money matters. When salespeople put off money discussions until too late in the process they waste time with prospects who are excited about the product and how they "could see it working for them" or how they would "love to have it" but once they find out the cost, don't have the ability to purchase it.

Failure to discuss money is also a major source of miscommunication between prospect and salesperson. Salespeople often think, "They know we are expensive and that we are worth every penny. They see the value. I think we can charge $10,000." Meanwhile the prospect has a different view: "This product (or service) can really help. I think it will fit in my $5,000 budget but hope I can get it for $4,000."

Besides wasting time and causing miscommunication, money weaknesses result in a myriad of other problems such as money left on the table, low margins, upset prospects, and excess pressure on the delivery team who have to deliver quality goods with minimal funds. The Optimal Salesperson is very comfortable talking about money and usually initiates the discussion early in the sales cycle, as discussed in Chapter 12.

Non-supportive Buy Cycle

Processes used in making a major personal purchase are predictive of how a salesperson will react in a selling situation. For example, when buying a 63" flat screen TV, salesperson Ted will do research, visiting four or five stores comparing prices, features, and functions, looking for the lowest price. When he thinks he knows where he will buy, he'll go back two or three times before signing on the dotted line. This process is referred to as buy cycle.

David Kurlan, president of the Objective Management Group, inc. proved that if a salesperson has this type of buy cycle, they will be vulnerable to prospects who want to put them through a similar process. If a prospect wants to comparison shop, a salesperson with a weak or non-supportive buy cycle will tolerate the behavior even if they have been taught the skills to ask the right questions to get the prospect to stop shopping.

However, salespeople with non-supportive buy cycles can still sell value – after all, not everyone comparison shops. Sometimes the urgency is just too great to shop. The Optimal Salesperson makes quick (not rash) decisions when buying and hence will be less vulnerable to buyers who are apt to put them through a bidding war. Chapter 14 will cover the buy cycle in more detail.

PART II

MOTIVATE YOURSELF

THE OPTIMAL SALESPERSON

4

Develop a Compelling
Reason to Succeed

Action is required to meet any goal. The primary reason to set a goal is to have a sufficient reason to take the actions that generate sales. Unfortunately, many times the goals set by the salespeople are ineffective and fail to compel the salesperson to take enough of the right actions to generate the level of sales required to be successful. As mentioned in Chapter 3, dramatic growth is achieved only by overcoming hidden weaknesses, which requires the expenditure of emotional energy as well as physical action. The Optimal Salesperson will set the type of goals that will motivate them personally to overcome weaknesses and achieve success.

SELL YOURSELF ON YOUR GOALS

The process of setting goals includes "selling" oneself on achieving success. The emotional energy the Optimal Salesperson invests is the "cost" of achieving that success.

Quotas are good examples of impotent goals. Management does not sit around saying, "You know … Martha is a great person. I think she deserves a better lifestyle. Let's set her quota so that if she reaches it, she can afford a bigger house." More likely, management will say, "What is the minimum we need from Martha to keep her on the payroll?" A seasoned salesperson who sets a goal to meet quota is likely to experience limited growth and probably won't have enough money to meet all of their (or their family's) personal goals. Conversely a person who can meet all of their personal goals by hitting quota probably won't have the motivation to do much more, no matter what "incentives" management puts in place.

So you'll need to create a personal vision of the future that will provide you with the necessary motivation to fight through the barriers on your way to success. Just as a successful real estate agent will paint a mental or even physical picture of the homeowner actually living in the house they're trying to sell, the Optimal Salesperson will create a picture of their perfect future with them in a starring role. Only then will they have something they can commit to and can compel them to take enough action to reach the goal.

BE SPECIFIC

Be specific when setting compelling goals. What exactly do I want; which model; what size; how many; how expensive; how much; anything in your vision that can be quantified should be spelled out. It is not enough to want a bigger house. You should specify how many rooms or how many acres. When setting goals, avoid trying to determine what is possible. Suspend disbelief for a while and dream of what would really motivate you to launch into massive action. You can inject a (small) dose of reality later.

Obviously goals set too far out of your current comfort zone can be de-motivating but goals that are too reachable will likely not move you at all. If there is some state of being that you crave, but which seems unreachable, keep the goal and change the time frame. For example, Mike really wanted a 40-foot fishing boat so he could relax next summer. But after specifying the details and estimating the cost, it seemed totally out of the question. By changing his time horizon from next summer to three years from now, he got fired up by the possibility and threw himself into the quest. If he has just said, "Someday I'll have a big boat…," he would have continued to poke along at his current, less than stellar, rate of sales.

"FEEL" THE GOAL

Logic by itself is insufficient to compel action. It's not enough to write down that your goal is to earn $20,000 more per year because your son has to go to college in a few years. You must "feel" the goal at a deeper level. You need to become emotionally involved with the goal if it is to move you to action.

Ask yourself why you want higher education for your son; what happens if he doesn't go; how will you feel if you have to tell him you can't afford it; how will you feel if he qualifies for admission to an Ivy League school and you can only pay for a state-supported school. If you find that you will feel like a failure or that you can't face your son if you can't afford his college, you are more likely to get out of your comfort zone and sell more and harder. But if your feeling is "It's no big deal if I don't earn the money because I had to pay my own way, and it will ultimately be good for him to take care of his own college expense and, besides, Ivy League schools are overrated." then the goal will not compel you to action. It will be a "nice to have" instead of a growth motivator.

BE SELFISH

Selfishness compels action. Because self-preservation is a basic instinct, self-interest is the greatest motivator. In the above example, your feelings are moving you to action but your son is getting the benefit.

We are not talking about the type of selfishness where you put yourself first every time. If anything, it's the reverse; you are making sure your loved ones get what they want before you fulfill your own needs. But most importantly, you are becoming emotionally involved with both your goals and theirs. Get in touch with how you will feel when you can provide what they want and how excited will you be when you reach your own goal.

Three things are essential when maximizing your motivation:

1. The priority must be correct (first theirs, then yours).

2. You must take responsibility for the goal.

3. You must become emotionally involved with the goal.

Once you have done all three, you will have successfully "sold" yourself on your goal.

STAY SOLD ON YOUR GOALS

Who hasn't made a New Year's resolution and then broken it? At the end of each year, millions of people set goals and resolve to meet them. Less than a month later, the goals and resolutions are forgotten. Weight loss companies know this and plan a major part of their ad budget for the first two weeks in January. If you want to avoid falling victim to losing sight of your goals and the motivation they provide, you must stay connected to those goals and, more importantly, to the emotional content behind them.

Write everything down and review it regularly. Also reduce the goals to a series of pictures that evoke the emotions that motivate you. Then put the pictures where you can see them every day -- your desk, your bedroom, even the screen saver on your computer. Soon you will stop consciously noticing the pictures but they will continue to work on you subconsciously. To maximize your growth and to minimize the time it will take you to achieve success, you'll need to stay connected to your vision and why it is important to you.

ESTABLISH METRICS AND MILESTONES

The completion date is the most important metric to set for a goal. A detailed description of what you want, why you want it, and how you will feel when you finally get it without a completion date is no goal at all. It is just a theoretical description of an end state. Dates drive action. Did you ever notice that six months before the end of a labor contract nothing happens? The closer the date gets, the more emotionally involved the participants become. Activity increases in inverse proportion to how many days are left in the contract. During the last few days people are meeting around the clock, pressure builds both internally and externally. No one wants to fail and look bad. The biggest movements occur when the time pressure caused by the end date is greatest.

You can do the same with personal goals. If there is no deadline, there will be no pressure to do anything different right now. You can stay in your comfort zone and don't have to grow. Without a set date, there will be no pressure to do anything differently than you have always done. And, as the saying goes, "If you always do what you have always done, you will always get what you've always got."

Milestone dates are equally important. The mind can't always connect actions today with an end date that is too far off in the future. Compare goal achievement with a cross-country auto trip. If I start from New York on Monday and need to be in Los Angeles by Saturday, that will dictate my rate of speed. If it's Friday and I am only as far as Ohio, I am in trouble. The prudent traveler will know where he needs to be at the end of each day's travel in order to arrive in Los Angeles as scheduled.

Similarly, the Optimal Salesperson will know what she must achieve each quarter, each month, and each week if she is to make the goal. Intermediate milestones will allow continuous awareness of your progress. They will also maintain a sense of urgency and drive action each day that creates movement towards the goal.

The ability to be measured is the key attribute of a useful milestone. To say that you must "make significant progress each day" is not very useful. The word "significant" is vague and varies from situation to situation. Driving 250 miles per day is significant progress but it won't get me to Los Angeles in a week. Being "better at handling objections" is also somewhat nebulous and hard to measure.

Therefore, milestones should be objective, with time periods natural to the cycle of your business. For instance, with a two year sales cycle, monthly goals are more useful than daily goals. On the other hand, daily goals may be more appropriate with a short sales cycle.

ESTABLISH AND USE A GOALS MANAGEMENT PROGRAM

"Decide" is a word taken from the Greek word meaning "to cut off from." When you truly decide something, you cut yourself off from all other options. "Deciding" on a goal is to set that as the only possibility. But a goal is not a goal until a date is set and you are emotionally involved in its achievement. So whenever you are frustrated with your current situation or excited about achieving a new, higher state of being is a good time to set a goal and begin your goals management program. When you are in this mindset, do it NOW!

If you wait, you may miss the opportunity and never get it back. So once you "decide" what you want, take action. As author and professional motivator Tony Robbins says, "never leave the scene of a decision without taking action." This includes writing the goal down, setting a date, and recording your feelings about why the goal is important to you. Your self-defeat mechanism may tell you to "do it next week," but don't let that happen. Carpe Diem! Seize the day, make the decision, set the goal, write it down and take the first step.

Of course you could be like everyone else and begin your goals program by the calendar at the beginning of a month, quarter, or year. This method can be effective but the emotion required may or may not be there when it is time to start.

Constant awareness of the goal is an important element of any goals management process. You'll need this awareness to guide your day-to-day actions to ensure that they are directed toward meeting your goal. Again, once you have "decided" on a goal, you've have eliminated other possibilities.

But awareness is not enough; goals require constant nurturing. You must regularly and consistently revisit the goals to review data, assess progress, analyze results, and extract information as well as learn lessons and adjust your approach. Review and evaluate your goals at set intervals such as weekly, monthly or quarterly or on the occasion of significant events like a big win or loss or revision of a commission plan.

Reviews should be done using the same or similar methods so that you can measure progress over a considerable period of time. For example, you might review sales activity trends weekly but only dig into pipeline trends monthly. Develop your own rhythm but remember that a little extra review is better than not enough.

PREPARE FOR SEA CHANGES

Visions change, sometimes abruptly and without warning. This is a healthy sign of growth. Work toward it. Expect it. Welcome it. When your vision changes, it is time to go through the whole goal-setting process all over again; even if it is in the middle of the year or month. For example, co-author Dan began his career with a goal of being president of a division of his company. He worked hard, acquired credentials, built his resume, and in time was short-listed as being promoted to that level in the next five years. However, one day after prolonged exposure to his desired position, he suddenly realized that being president wasn't all it was cracked up to be, not only in terms of compensation but in the type of work involved.

Dan revised his goals and redirected his efforts and within three months had embarked on a new career as a self-employed sales force development consultant. He set a different path that could lead him to his new goals, one that helped him reach them in an extremely short period of time.

When you set a goal with an accomplish-by date, you will either succeed or fail. There's no in-between. When the inevitability of success or failure becomes apparent, it is time once again to go through the whole goal-setting process. Don't wait until the next regularly scheduled review. Do it NOW so as not to waste any time you could be devoting to accomplish the new goal.

THINK ABOUT YOUR GOALS

Be thoughtful when setting goals. Although there is no standard on how often you should change them, revising them every time there is a shift in the workplace or its trends shows a lack of commitment.   Resist the urge to adjust goals every time something happens in the market or company. You might adjust your approach or activity level but the goals should remain consistent until they are achieved, you prove to yourself that you can't do it, or your wants and desires actually change. If you feel the need to make a change, review why you wanted the vision in the first place and ask yourself why you feel differently now. Questions may include:

- Why don't I want the goal anymore? Be specific.

- Why do I want this now? Does it have to do with me personally or external factors?

- What caused me to change my mind?

Again, try to find a particular cause or reasons. Honest answers will give you new or renewed direction and motivation.

BURN YOUR EMOTIONAL BOATS

When attacking a foreign land, ancient warriors came ashore and then promptly burned the boats that brought them. This would ensure total commitment to success in battle, since retreat was not an option. Although of course it's foolish to risk life, limb, or financial ruin, nobody ever died from being told "no!

Therefore, put your whole self into the effort. It's OK to risk being rejected by asking a tough question or getting a response you really don't want to hear. The moment you are willing to accept the rejection or the repercussion is the moment you are fully committed to the goal and have burned your "emotional boats." You should also make sure your vision is big and important enough to be worth committing to and burning the boat for. If the vision is too small you will stay in your comfort zone and remain stuck at your current level.

WORK THROUGH FEAR OF FAILURE

Acceptance of failure is a part of the growth process. No one succeeds all the time. Hall of Fame baseball players have an average overall failure rate of seven out of ten times at bat. Rather than being feared, failure is just part of the process. When you do fail – and you probably will, sometime before you reach your final goal -- analyze what happened, learn from the experience, adjust your approach if necessary, and try again. If you have a compelling enough reason to succeed, are "sold" on the ultimate vision and committed to success, then some failure is easier to accept and should be considered as part of the journey.

5

Stoke the Fires of Personal Motivation

All motivation is personal motivation. Even when we are seemingly motivated to meet corporate goals, we are usually doing it for personal reasons such as recognition, loyalty to a mentor, hope of receiving a bonus, and so forth.

Motivation comes from within a person and cannot be "done" to someone. Charismatic speakers such as politicians, evangelists, sales trainers, business leaders, coaches and popular athletes are sometimes described as motivators and often earn large fees as speakers. But the truth is they are skilled at tapping into an emotion or desire that already exists within the audience. They don't actually create motivation. Most often what they create is excitement which is usually short-lived.

THE IMPORTANCE OF DESIRE

<u>Desire</u> is an emotion that moves us inexorably forward toward something we don't have now -- money, material

possessions, peace of mind, security, and so on. It is often described as a fire burning within or a fire in the belly. Desire is innate though it is often unrecognized or suppressed.

Desire is the single most important attribute of the Optimal Salesperson and is crucial to their growth. Without desire, stagnation sets in. Desire is irreplaceable; no other skill can be a substitute. Desire is also innate -- you either have it or you don't. It can, however, change over time. Many times, achieving a goal lessens desire; we become satisfied and lose our drive to go further.

<u>Passion</u> is a facet of desire. There is a world of difference between wanting something and being passionate about it. If I merely want more money or need it, I can be talked out if it without too much trouble. But if I am passionate about achieving a certain state, nothing will stand in my way because I am emotionally invested in achievement of the goal. Many people who lived through the Great Depression of the 1930s were passionate about paying off mortgages in the 1950s and 1960s as soon as possible because they witnessed people who owed money to the bank lose their homes. They were emotionally invested in not owing anybody anything.

Optimal Salespeople are passionate about their goals; failure is not an option. They are emotionally invested in their objectives and are driven to fight through obstacles that stand between them and their goals. All too often in sales, excitement dies with the first rejection. Optimal Salespeople work through that rejection and use it as a steppingstone towards success.

Own the Goal

Half-hearted efforts by salespeople can usually be traced back to the salesperson not "owning" the goal. If you don't own the goal it means you were not sold on the idea of achieving the goal in the first place. When selling anything to anybody, there needs to be a compelling reason to proceed or no sale will be made. This applies even to selling oneself. That is why we like to talk about achieving a vision rather than achieving goals. It is easier to identify a compelling reason to achieve a certain lifestyle than to sell 32 widgets this month. If there is no compelling reason, there will be no passion and no emotional involvement with achieving the vision.

When setting goals, step back and ask yourself objective questions that will test your level of desire For example, ask yourself:

- Why do I want that?

- What happens if I don't get it?

- What will it do for me?

- How will I feel when I succeed?

- How will I feel if I fail?

Tepid answers usually indicate that you have selected a vision that doesn't excite you sufficiently to propel you through any obstacles you may encounter along the way.

Life Changes and the Price of Success

If you do achieve success and the vision, you may wonder, what next? You can revise the vision upwards to include more, bigger, and better everything or you can change your focus. Instead of more money for themselves, Optimal Salespeople have focused on giving back to their community. They adopt a charity; they commit time to helping others, which can be even more motivating than trying to get more for yourself.

Regardless of whatever new goals you set for yourself, you'll still need to grow and push through emotional barriers to sell more, take less time selling the same amount, or apply your selling skills to whatever cause you adopt. The Optimal Salesperson constantly challenges himself or herself to grow by identifying bigger and better visions of the future to which they can become emotionally involved and passionate about.

But what if the flame is extinguished and you lose passion for your vision? This can and does happen: at certain stages in life, you and your family may realize you have everything you ever wanted and have enough resources to give back to the community. Or you can lose a spouse or partner or contract a major disease. Sometimes it is time to focus on other things.

Even if these do occur, you need to be accountable. If you're still working, make sure you meet the requirements of your job and your boss's expectations. And recognize that you are making a conscious decision to lower your goals and activity plans. Communicate your decision to relevant parties so they know what to expect.

COMMITMENT COMPLIMENTS DESIRE

Simply put, <u>commitment</u> is a measure of the sacrifice you are willing to make to achieve your personal goal. Commitment is as essential to the growth of the Optimal Salesperson as desire and, as mentioned in Chapter 4, these two are opposite sides of the motivation coin.

Commitment involves more than working long hours or even working "smart," although both are important. Rather commitment involves an <u>emotional</u> sacrifice. Even though it might be hard to ask a prospect a tough question, you are willing to do so anyway, even if it is difficult to hear the answer. You are willing to step out of your comfort zone and make cold calls or ask for referrals, because you believe in your vision. You are even willing to handle rejection, and avoid making excuses not to prospect.

The Optimal Salesperson continually makes these sacrifices until they become part of his or her comfort zone. They are willing to do so because they know that desire without commitment is just wishful thinking.

Limit Your Options

Too many options can lead to stagnation. If I have the option of either asking about money on a call or not asking, I can come up with a reason for avoiding the question and staying in my comfort zone. "It was not the right time." "He was focused on something else." "I didn't want to upset her," and so on. The secret to commitment is to leave yourself no options. For example, our physical makeup is such that we have no option about breathing: It is either breathe or die within a minute or two. Of course, the sales profession does not entail life and death on a minute-by-minute basis. Though it may seem life-threatening when we confront our inner fears, no one dies from a bad sales call. And to force growth, sometimes we need to artificially create a situation that has dire consequences. We need to make required actions mandatory and do the thing we fear the most.

Enlisting the help of those closest to you can also help stretch your comfort zone. If, for example, you are having trouble asking for referrals, confide your fear in your spouse or significant other and promise that you will ask five people during the next week. The authors have used this technique to spur each other's growth. You will not want to disappoint your spouse/significant other by failing to do something totally within your control; your commitment to them is usually stronger than your fear. You may fail a time or two, but an understanding spouse will support and encourage you to try again, and soon you should be able to break through whatever barrier is holding you back. Colleagues, mentors, and sales coaches can also be useful in much the same way.

OUTLOOK, THE FORCE MULTIPLIER

Attitude about the state of the world around us is referred to as <u>outlook</u>. The Optimal Salesperson has an optimistic view of things while others take a "glass half-empty" approach. A positive outlook in and of itself is not enough to ensure success. Rather, it acts like a force multiplier. When a person is in a positive frame of mind they are more likely to take action. Obstacles appear minor; goals appear within reach, positive outcomes are assumed, and tasks are attacked with an air of confidence and an expectation of success. This mindset allows our natural skills to take effect and minimizes our weaknesses. If the positive outlook remains intact, failures are seen as minor setbacks on the road to success. Winners, whether in sports, business, or the arts, when interviewed after a major triumph, almost always give the same quote: "I knew I could do it; I just stayed positive, worked hard and overcame the obstacles." You never hear them say, "I don't know how this happened. I never thought I could do it, I gave up hope half way through but somehow luck came through for me."

Similarly, a negative outlook can adversely affect your efforts. When the economy is weak, many salespeople say to themselves, "Nobody is buying; it doesn't matter what I say. What's the use of calling people?" Since they are resigned to a negative outcome, they may not even make the attempt. If they do go out and try to do their job, their efforts will often be half-hearted with an expectation of failure. Small obstacles will be magnified in their own mind and seen as proof of what they feared, thus reinforcing the negative outlook. It becomes a vicious cycle. A negative attitude leads to weak effort that yields poor results that lead to an even worse attitude.

Motivation -- the combination of desire and commitment -- will outweigh the effects of a negative attitude as long as the salesperson is sufficiently "sold" on the goals they set for themselves. Without a sufficiently compelling reason to succeed, you will be swamped by the negative attitude and motivation will disappear entirely, thus stifling your growth. On the other hand, a positive attitude will magnify your desire and commitment, because it is easier to be committed to a course of action when success seems assured.

An important point is that outlook is independent of reality. A person can, and should, have a positive outlook even when the actual environment is far less than ideal.

For example, as of this writing the real estate market is in bad shape, with no relief in sight. A Realtor with a negative outlook has the following self-talk: "No one is buying, listings aren't selling, competition is steep, nothing is working; what's the use...." Someone with this attitude will give a half-hearted effort at best. Most successful Realtors will have something like the following mindset: "Sales are down dramatically but they are far from zero. I'm in a market area where typically 250 houses are sold every month. I only need to sell five to meet my goals. Even if the market were down 60 percent I should still be able to find five houses to sell. With things this bad, other Realtors are quitting and no new ones are entering the market. This is a great time to increase my market share. I better get to work before the market improves and my window of opportunity closes." It is easy to imagine how this attitude will affect this Realtor's day-to-day behavior.

NO EXCUSES!

Responsibility works in much the same way as outlook. It will affect motivation by either supporting or diminishing it. By <u>responsibility</u> we mean the willingness to be accountable for results or lack of thereof. The Optimal Salesperson does not make excuses for less than favorable outcomes. They don't blame the economy or the operations department or management or the competition. They realize that they pretty much control their own destiny. If a down economy means fewer prospects in the marketplace, then they adjust by making more calls or stepping up their referral program. If the operations department fails to support them in some way, they realize that maybe they didn't give them enough lead time or failed to communicate effectively. If the competition undercuts their price, they review their own approach to determine how they could have emphasized the value of their solution to the prospect. The Optimal Salesperson accepts responsibility for a failure; changes his/her own approach where necessary; and moves on to the next prospect.

Adjusting to a changing environment is key to survival and ultimate success. Excuse-makers cede control of the outcome to outside factors, rendering them powerless to control their own destiny. If you don't acknowledge your role in a failed outcome, there will be no need to adjust your approach, improve a skill, or put any effort into overcoming a self-limiting belief. This inaction will cause stagnation to set in and stunt your growth. If this pattern of excuse-making continues, the salesperson will begin to wallow in self-pity as they bemoan their situation in that bad things continually happen to them. This can cause or amplify a negative outlook and add to a vicious cycle of failure.

Self-reliance is enhanced in those who routinely accept responsibility for all outcomes, both positive and negative. Accepting responsibility causes the Optimal Salesperson to have to stretch the limits of their capabilities and beyond. They build new sales "muscles" when they find ways to defeat the obstacles thrown up by their environment. If the operations department can't support them they figure out how to advance the sale without them. If their prices are higher, they have to increase their skills in selling value.

"So how do you tell the difference between an excuse and a really good reason?" You may ask. The answer is both frustrating and challenging: They are all excuses. Yes, the economy really is bad, the competition really did buy the deal, the operations manager is really out to get you, and so forth. But the Optimal Salesperson evaluates the environment and finds ways to work around any obstacles. Even when something unexpected happens, they realize that maybe they should have foreseen it and take steps not to be surprised in this way again.

A good parallel is a football team. Excessive injuries sometimes occur that can affect the team's chances of winning a title. A winning coach will take responsibility for the losses that follow the injuries by hiring more skilled or versatile backup players, changing the practice routine, upgrading the strength and conditioning of the players, eliminating injury prone players, making different substitutions or even re-sodding the playing field. The losing mentality is to make the excuse that injuries are out of his control that no action on his part is required. The Optimal Salesperson never makes excuses, even if such excuses seem warranted.

Accepting responsibility almost always causes Optimal Salespeople to take some action that moves them to a new place -- both literally and figuratively -- that promotes growth and leads to successful outcomes.

PART III

THE TOOLS OF THE OPTIMAL
SALESPERSON

6

Design a Sales Activity Plan and Track Daily Progress

Getting salespeople to implement a sales activity plan and tracking system can be extremely difficult. However, it's surprisingly easy to execute and pays huge dividends. The tracking system described in this chapter should take about a half-hour to set up and then no more than 15 minutes a week to maintain. Developing a sales activity plan and tracking progress will eliminate slumps, allow you to diagnose problems, and give you a feeling of accomplishment. Tracking can also improve confidence and provide reassurance that your next sale is imminent. You play sports with more intensity when you keep score. Similarly, you'll work harder when you track your sales activity.

WHAT IS A SALES ACTIVITY PLAN?

<u>Sales activities</u> are actions that lead directly to sales. Sales activities include (but are not limited to) talking to prospects,

booking appointments, asking for referrals, attending networking meetings, and making cold calls.

Other behaviors indirectly related to sales are known as <u>sales-related activities</u>. They include preparing forecasts, updating prospect files, attending sales meetings, training, preparing marketing materials, and so on. Since it is never a crisis to make a sales call and since sales-related activities usually have deadlines, unfortunately many if not most salespeople find themselves devoting too much time to sales-related activities and not enough to sales activities themselves.

A <u>sales activity plan</u> is an estimate of the level of sales activity required to reach a particular sales goal. <u>Tracking</u> is a method used to measure the actual level of sales activity. Tracking sales activity allows the Optimal Salesperson to compare actual to planned activity and make adjustments to his or her daily workload, ensuring that the goal is achieved.

WHY HAVE A SALES ACTIVITY PLAN?

Perhaps the most important argument for a sales activity plan comes from the salespeople themselves. Consider Dave's story below.

Case Study: Dave

Dave was an associate real estate broker who earned about $120,000 per year in commissions. He had successfully implemented an effective sales process and worked diligently to eliminate most of his self-limiting beliefs. He set goals faithfully; however, he refused to create a sales activity plan to track his progress, despite repeated attempts by his coach (co-author Dan) to get him to do so.

Then one day Dave realized he had been sidetracked during the previous four months and had closed only one small deal during that time. He came to Dan and requested help in getting back up to two deals per month, about half of his prior rate. Dan agreed to help but only if Dave would make a plan and track progress. Dave agreed very reluctantly.

However, within a month Dave was back to his former sales rate, exceeding his lowered expectations. Over the next year he doubled his income and the following year, doubled it again. Dave attributed his meteoric rise to the discipline that tracking brought to his sales career. Managing his selling effort resulted in him becoming an Optimal Salesperson.

Salespeople who fail to implement an activity plan may fall prey to consultant's wiggle, a description of the results of the unsuccessful salesperson, depicted in Figure 6.1. Imagine Mark, the consultant, who goes into business for himself at Point A. He has no business, so all he does is make sales calls until he finds a project to work on. He is then at Point B, earning money and way too busy to make sales calls. Eventually the project ends and he finds himself at Point C, back where he started with nothing to do but make sales calls.

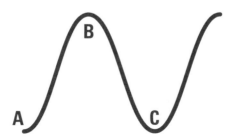

Figure 6.1. Consultant's Wiggle.

Unsuccessful salespeople follow this same pattern; lots of sales activity, followed by no sales activity while they are distracted with paperwork and proposals, then more frantic sales activity as they scramble to find prospects and so goes the cycle over and over.

The Optimal Salesperson has a plan that specifies sales activities required to meet sales goals and how much of each activity should be performed in each time period (day, week, month, and so on). When the required activities are specified and the level of effort defined, related but non-sales activities (proposals, forecasts, expense reports, call reports) can be fit in and around the critical sales activity, ensuring that income-sustaining sales activities actually get done.

WHAT CAN (AND CAN'T) I MANAGE?

<u>Control</u> is a critical factor in the management of anything. If you can't control it you can't manage it. Some people disagree with this principle and those people we assign as manager of sun spots. There is no way for them to succeed as manager of sun spots. They can monitor sun spots and track them, but they can't manage them because they have no control over sun spots. Another is sales revenue, because you have no control over the customer actually placing the order. You can't make a person reach into his or her pocket and give you money. The only things you can manage in sales are what you do and say and how you react to others. So you put the tasks you can control and manage day-to-day into your sales activity plan. These include attempts to contact a prospect, sales conversations, appointments booked, qualified opportunities uncovered, quotes, and sales closed. There might be a few others such as demonstrations performed or referrals received. But 80-

90 percent of sales activity plans are primarily focused on the activities listed below.

- *Attempts* – Dialing the telephone or walking into a prospect's office. We generally don't count text messages or e-mails sent since these usually are ways for salespeople to avoid rejection but there have been exceptions..

- *Conversations* – A discussion (no matter how short or effective) in person or by phone where the intent is to generate interest in a product or service and to schedule an appointment to talk about it in more detail.

- *Booked Appointment* – When the prospect actually schedules time to meet. This is usually in person but could be a Web meeting or phone call if distance is an issue.

- *Qualified Opportunities Uncovered* – These usually result from one or more appointments that determine whether the prospect meets all of the criteria to be considered qualified in accordance with the sales process.

- *Quotes* – A formal submittal or an informal proposal.

- *Sales* – When the prospect says "yes" and money changes hands or a purchase order is generated.

CREATING A SALES ACTIVITY PLAN

Sales activity plans begin with the financial goals of the salesperson and company. You then work backwards to arrive at the activity required to meet the financial goals. The most complex plan should take no more than half an hour to prepare. If you haven't been tracking, you may not have metrics at hand, such as closing rates of proposals and conversation rates of cold calls to appointments. So, you should use a SWAG (scientific will ass guess) or PFA (picked from air) numbers.

When creating the plan, remember three things. You are looking for a level of effort; ratios will change as you get better or the market conditions change; and after you track for a while you will have the actual metrics and can adjust. You can fine-tune the plan as you go along. The most important thing, especially in the beginning, is to get it done quickly so you can get started with the activities. The example below describes how you can use figures to precisely track sales activity and sales goals.

Case Study: Lena

Lena sells pumps to industrial clients. She must earn $100,000 to meet her financial goals and the company's sales goal for her is $2 million per year. The average order is $200,000, which gives her $4,000 in commission. She is paid a $52,000 salary. Therefore, to meet her personal goal she must make 12 sales this year to earn $48,000 in commission. That puts her 20 percent above her company's sales goal ($2.4 million vs. $2 million). At her closing rate of 50 percent on proposals made, she must make 24 quotes. To get 24 quotes she must find 30 qualified opportunities to pursue since 15-20 percent drop out along the way for one reason or another. To find 30 qualified opportunities she needs first appointments with 100 prospects to talk about new projects, since about one third of the prospects she meets for the first time either don't have the appropriate need or enough money to make them a qualified prospect. To get 100 appointments she must talk to 400 people at a conversation rate of 25 percent. Most of her appointments are set up by phone and she estimates that she connects with a decision-maker one out of four times she dials the phone. Thus her sales activity plan would look like the chart below.

	Year	Month*	Week*
Dials	1,600	130	30
Conversations	400	35	8
1st Appointments	100	8	2
Qualified Opportunities	30	3	1
Proposals	24	.5	.13
Sales #	12	1	.25
Sales $	$2,400,000	$200,000	$50,000
Commission $	$48,000	$4,000	$1,000
*Some numbers rounded off – 50 weeks/year			

WHY TRACK ACTIVITY?

Measurement drives action; what gets measured gets done. Tracking essential sales activity puts results at the forefront of awareness. If you are committed to tracking your activity you won't be able to "forget" to make calls. Tracking will cause you to work harder and prioritize your activity correctly. It also helps diagnose and pinpoint problem areas. For example, at the quarterly review it was discovered Lena's sales were behind plan. She had enough appointments but not enough qualified opportunities. Her manager was able to conclude that she needed a refresher on how to qualify prospects; she could have been calling too low in the organization. But a review of her prospect list eliminated that possibility and revealed that she wasn't asking the right questions. By tracking Lena's activity, the manager knew where to start looking for the cause of the problem and was more readily able help her correct it.

Tracking Sales Activity

"Track daily, report weekly, and analyze monthly" is a formula for using a sales activity tracking system that will spur personal growth and help ensure that sales goals are met. Although you should record the number of calls, conversations with decision-makers, and appointments booked, for tracking purposes there's no need to write extensive reports of their content or outcome. Documenting the essence of the conversations is important for legal and contractual purposes but that is more properly the purview of a Customer Relationship Management (CRM) rather than a sales activity tracking system.

Each time an Optimal Salesperson initiates a particular sales activity, she makes a tick mark in a scorecard which she always keeps handy. At the end of the day, the scorecard is totaled and the results tabulated. At the end of the week, the results are recorded and sent to the manager, either manually or via technology. As the data is tabulated and recorded each week, it can be compared to the planned activity to make sure that enough activity has been generated and that the assumed ratios are holding. Simple awareness of the level of a particular activity is usually enough to keep a salesperson on pace to meet goals.

Recording your activity is the most important thing, rather than defining precise numbers. If you forget to mark down a call here or there it doesn't matter as long as you are consistent. If you get 85-90 percent of the data right, you will gain valuable insight into your selling behavior and understanding of your level of effort. Also, ratios change over time as skills improve. So don't waste a lot of energy trying to be too precise. Just be honest with yourself, track consistently, and review the data regularly.

Consistent tracking leads to consistent activity and consistent activity leads to consistent and dependable results. There is nothing more frustrating for a salesperson or manager than sales results that vary wildly form month to month and quarter to quarter, 140 percent of quota one time followed by 10 percent the next time. Use of a sales activity plan and a tracking system will eliminate most of this variation and make forecasting much more reliable.

Bringing problem areas to the surface quickly is another result of a good tracking system. Activity data can pinpoint problem areas much more quickly. Once the relationship between activity and results is clearly understood and documented, the tracking system can expose problems the salesperson may be having with both sales process issues as well as self-limiting belief issues.

Using Sales Activity for Growth

However, sales activity numbers are meaningless unless someone takes the time to analyze data and turn it into information. Information is only useful if it gives you insight into cause and effect and can aid you in altering your course of action to keep you on track. For example, consider Gene in the case study below.

Case Study: Gene

Gene is a seasoned insurance salesperson who uses a two-call closing system. The first call is qualifying and data gathering and the second is to deliver a quote if the prospect qualifies and to close the sale. He reports that for the last eight weeks his number of first calls, second calls and sales are as follows: 8/2/2, 9/3/2, 7/2/2, 8/2/2, 8/7/2, 8/8/1, 8/8/2, and 8/8/1. In plain English, the first week he had eight first calls, two times he delivered a quote, and two times he sold the policy. Reviewing the numbers, Gene's manager noticed that beginning in the fifth week Gene went from closing nearly everyone he quoted to closing one out of four or so. What happened to cause the change?

After an in-depth discussion and debriefing, the manager gleaned from Gene that he was not qualifying his prospects properly. Competition was stiffening due to changing market conditions and Gene had resorted to quoting everyone he saw. The result was actually a reduction in closing rate and actual sales.

The manager was able to coach Gene to adjust his mindset and get back to using his sales process and only quoting qualified prospects. The key factor here is that the manager focused his attention on changes in the numbers, trends, and ratios. The absolute values were not as important as the changes themselves which helped gain insight and adjust behavior.

Consider this kind of tracking as a sort of "Check Engine" light that goes on in your car. You may not want to see it because it usually means a trip to the shop. But you know to either take corrective action or drive at your own peril. Sales activity data functions in exactly the same manner. When activity drops and closing ratios fail to increase, even the mathematically-challenged can deduce a future slump unless steps are taken to get activity back to where it needs to be. Monitoring of sales activity acts like an early warning signal that spurs action and keeps the Optimal Salesperson on track to achieve goals.

Using Sales Activity to Find Hidden Obstacles

After a period of time, tracking sales activity also helps detect self-limiting beliefs, hidden weakness, and skill deficiencies. It enables you to catch these flaws before they develop into big problems, as was the case with Brian below.

Case Study: Brian

Brian made a very large sale in May. It represented about four month's worth of normal sales and made both Brian and his manager very happy. It looked like Brian would finally be able to take his place among the elite salespeople in the company. However, at the end of June Brian noticed that the number of appointments booked during the month was 50 percent less than what he had been averaging over the past two years. What had changed? he wondered.

He knew he had some additional administrative work in connection with such a large sale; but after thinking about it further, he realized he'd become complacent and lost focus on his goals. He had taken too much time off from prospecting (the hard work of sales) and had contracted a classic case of "Rest-on-one's-laurelitis." Having recognized the problem, Brian was able to work harder in July and avoided a precipitous drop in sales.

DEBUNKING EXCUSES FOR NOT TRACKING

Time spent keeping track of calls is time better spent making calls." This is the battle cry of opponents to tracking activity. However, if you follow the guidelines in this chapter, you only save about 15 minutes a week by not tracking. That's less than what most people take for a coffee break! Also keeping track of your calls can motivate you to make more calls, especially if you don't make enough. So you'll likely be taking fewer breaks and making more calls if you track.

There are many reasons why people don't like to track their activities. Psychologically speaking, we have an internal mechanism that works to keep us in our comfort zone and makes growth such an arduous process. One of the easiest ways for this mechanism to keep us where we are is to avoid tracking at ill costs. So we tell ourselves that tracking is a waste of time; or the data doesn't mean anything; or it takes too long; anything to prevent us from doing what will help move us out of our comfort zone. Also, most salespeople are not numbers-oriented. They have difficulty deriving meaningful information from the data they collect so it seems like a waste of time. If you have real issues dealing with numbers, get your accountant or sales coach to analyze them for you.

Another excuse is "It's too much paperwork." However, putting a "tick" mark on a pad next to a phone is far from writing a detailed report on each person called or visited. All you need to do is track the number of calls, meetings, and proposals. This takes maybe 15 minutes at the end of the week to total them up and enter them into a report.

Sales managers make lots of excuses for not holding people accountable but the biggest concern is that the data are not reliable since the data are not verifiable. They believe salespeople can just "fudge" the data. In the very short term they are correct. The salesperson can report that they made 50 calls when they actually only made 10. They can report 10 face-to-face meetings when there were only 2. However, reporting the activity is only part of the sales management process. Skillful debriefing will uncover "faked" data.

On occasion over the last two decades we have encountered salespeople who have tried to get away with this, but in the short order they realize they are too easily unmasked and that in fact it is a lot of trouble to fake the reports. We have found that when a tracking system is put in place as part of an effective sales management system; the sales people either get better or get lost. Chief Executive Officers seeking to grow their companies should accept no excuses from sales managers for not tracking sales activity of the salespeople.

THE OPTIMAL SALESPERSON

7

Be a Prolific Prospector

Closing is overrated. If given a choice between a closer who can't prospect and a prolific prospector who can't close, we will take the prospector every time. Yet the ability to consistently generate enough of the right type of prospects to fill the pipeline without the aid of massive marketing dollars is relatively rare.

PROSPECTING YIELDS SALES GOLD

Although reams have been written about the latest selling process or about overall selling theory, not enough attention has been paid to developing the ability to prospect. Recently a national sales training organization even published a corporate training course which omitted prospecting from the curriculum altogether!

You first must have prospects before you can move them through a sales process or use any other sales skills. The Optimal Salesperson is a prolific prospector because they realize that it is the most important skill to have. You can't close anyone who is not in your pipeline in the first place.

Opportunity is everywhere but you have to look for it. Contrary to popular belief, opportunity doesn't actually knock; you have to see it, recognize it, and grab it by the throat. How often have you watched a colleague bring in a big sale and said to yourself "Why didn't I see that?" or "How did I miss that one?" The missing ingredient is often awareness or, in sales, <u>prospecting awareness</u>. You have to know what you are looking for, be a keen observer of your surroundings, and be willing to constantly interact with people around you.

There are many ways to prospect. Cold calling, networking, and getting referrals are the most popular. However you do it, prospecting is basically a sifting operation. Gold prospectors know what gold looks like, put themselves in the vicinity of it, and then sift through lots of stuff to find those nuggets that can make them rich. The Optimal Salesperson is not only prolific prospector; he is also an efficient one. And the most efficient way to prospect is to have people who are working to introduce you to the right people at the right time. Although this is the most efficient way to prospect, it is not the method over which you have the most control.

Cold calling holds that distinction. However, it also has the lowest success rate. The Optimal Salesperson prospects primarily by <u>introduction</u>.

INTRODUCTIONS ARE THE KEY

So how do you generate a steady stream of introductions and referrals? First, by establishing <u>trust</u>, which is 50-100 times more effective than making cold calls or following up leads. Distrust of salespeople in general is high to begin with, but distrust of salespeople who cold call a prospect is much greater than that. When a friend or trusted colleague introduces you to a salesperson, a large measure if the trust the prospect has for the referrer is transferred to the salesperson. Barriers disappear, genuine communication occurs, and closing rates skyrocket.

The difference between a referral and an introduction is largely a matter of control. A <u>referral</u> occurs if a client or friend gives your name to a friend and tells that friend to call you. This generally happens without your knowledge and the "prospect" may or may not actually contact you. You have no control over this process. Unscientific anecdotal evidence collected over the last 20 years or so suggests referrals of this type are effective 10-20 percent of the time.

A referral might also work the other way. Your client may tell you to call his friend because he thinks his friend "could use your help." In this case you have control but the conversion rates are still relatively low because the referral prospect doesn't know you, and the trust barrier is not as low as it could be.

An <u>introduction</u> occurs when your client talks to his friend and states that you can help with her problem. The client obtains permission for you to call the prospect, then calls you and describes the problem to you and gives you the name and phone number of the referral. Obviously this can also occur the old-fashioned way with an in-person introduction. When you receive an introduction to a prospect, trust is transferred and you have control of the situation. When you exclusively work with introductions, your prospecting time will be dramatically reduced.

HOW TO OBTAIN INTRODUCTIONS

The first step in getting introductions involves <u>expectation</u>. Not only should you anticipate getting introductions, but you should feel that you deserve them. Without this mindset, introductions will only happen sporadically and infrequently. Second, you must have a process in place to help you generate a <u>consistent stream</u> of introductions. The next several sections will outline an effective process. A third and equally important step is <u>effort</u>. Just as with other types of sales activities, generating a constant stream of high-quality introductions to the right people at the right time requires a consistent level of activity.

Identify Your Target Client

Most salespeople have a nebulous idea of who they are looking for. That makes prospecting a little like searching for a needle in a haystack without ever having seen a needle before.

So sit down and write a one-page description of your ideal client. This will help provide you with a clear picture of exactly what you are looking for. Describe your prospect in terms your referral source will be able to recognize (such as position in the company) and avoid criteria that referrers would have no way of knowing (such as net worth of $2 million). Descriptions should include the typical problems a prospect may have that you are able to address and the job title of person in the organization you would like to be introduced to. A sample of a target client description for the authors can be found in Figure 7.1. As you can see, the person we need to be introduced to is the President or CEO.

Target Clients for Caramanico Maguire Associates Salesforce Development

<u>What We Do</u>

- Evaluate the sales organization

- Align the people and processes with corporate goals

- Modify systems to promote growth

- Train those with growth potential

- Replace weak performers

<u>Indicators</u>

Our clients are companies with sales between $10-100 million with 5-30 sales people. They can be in either a product or a service business. They are in a growth mode and the president or CEO is struggling with how to take them to the next level. They may be having problems with:

- Turnover in the sales force

- Nonproductive salespeople

- Can't find the right people

- Too many quotes, not enough closing

- Ineffective sales management

- Hearing excuses while not getting results

Figure 7.1. Target Client Description

The Optimal Salesperson knows not to pursue unprofitable clients. Therefore, you need to spend time identifying them so you don't pursue the wrong ones. Prospects may also be undesirable for other reasons. For example, they may be too hard to close and take too much time or require too many resources (demos, tech resources, etc.). These are some of the reasons why Optimal Salespeople sometimes eliminate government organizations, large corporations, individuals, small companies, engineers, and others from their list of prospects.

SOURCES OF REFERRALS

<u>Clients</u> are your best source of introductions. Your best new clients will most likely come from your best existing clients. They know what you do and can vouch for your quality, delivery, and so on. In addition, you have most likely gone out of your way to help an existing client out of one difficulty or another. They have reason to want to help you. In fact they may already be telling people about you. If your phone isn't ringing, they probably don't know how to introduce you effectively. But you can help them with that.

<u>Centers of influence</u> are another excellent source of introductions and can include industry executives, published authors, and even Chamber of Commerce presidents. To be a center of influence, an individual must have a large network of contacts (the "center" part.) They must have some "influence" over them. So if centers of influence recommend something, people will act. However, beware of people who consider themselves "centers of influence." They may know everyone but nobody trusts them and therefore are not good sources for introductions.

It is also useful to find or develop a <u>referral partner</u>. This is someone with a service or product that compliments yours. You refer them and they refer you. Moving company and telephone system salespeople are a good example. Their client bases overlap but they don't sell competing products. Companies who are moving usually need new phone systems and companies often look into new phone systems when they begin thinking about moving.

APPROACHING INTRODUCTION SOURCES

<u>Asking for help</u> is the best way to approach someone who might be able to introduce you. A conversation with a trusted client might go like this:

You: "John, I was hoping you could help me out."

Client: "I'll try."

You: "I am trying to expand my client base. In the past, I have found that my best new clients came from my best existing clients. If you knew the right kind of people would you be willing to introduce me?'

Client: "Absolutely! In fact, has George Smith called you? I gave him your name last month."

You: "He hasn't called. But before you agree to help, can I give you a specific idea of what I am asking for? That way, we won't waste any of your valuable time "

Client: "No problem. What do you need?"

Treat the above as an approach and not a script. Your words will vary from situation to situation.

Notice that your client will now be able to tell exactly what you need and can either agree or refuse. A similar approach will work for referral partners and centers of influence.

Your <u>target client</u> is the first thing you want your introduction source to understand. Pull out the one-page description of the target client and go over it with the client. Ask them if they would mind introducing you to someone who might fit the description. If they say "yes," find out how many people they might be able to introduce you to over the next year. Answers usually range from one to six. Be careful of accepting too many referrals as they may feel pressure and not follow through.

You now have a general agreement as to what they can do for you. You can then provide further guidance:

You: "John, I have found that referrals work best if you phone them and they are expecting my call. I'm sure your colleague George intended to get back to me but became too busy or lost my number. How about in the future when someone expresses interest in talking to me, tell them you will have me call them and ask if that is okay. if they agree, you can let me know an then give me their number. Are you comfortable with that?"

Client: "Sounds good."

You: "Also, would you mind spending a few minutes over the next week or so to search your database and find one or two additional referrals? After that and again if you don't mind, I'll occasionally touch base to see how you are making out.

Client: "That sounds great! I'll do it tonight. "

You: "Thanks. I appreciate your help. I'll call in a couple of days to get the information."

Say you do this with 10 people. You could get a commitment of up to 60 ideal prospects in the pipeline over the next year, although the actual number would likely be half or possibly even a little less. Your workload after the initial meeting would consist of 10 calls to referrers per month plus the calls to the prospects. (First make sure the referring clients are OK with you calling them once a month; otherwise they might construe it as pestering.) Contrast that with the effort it takes to generate the same pipeline by making cold calls.

DEVELOP A STRONG NETWORK

Contacts are the lifeblood of prospecting. If you were born a Kennedy, Rockefeller, or Bush, you would have a Blackberry full of names and numbers of important people who would be happy to introduce you to anyone you needed to meet. Although most of us are not so lucky, there are other ways to acquire a large contact list. A common method is <u>networking</u>; the process of building and maintaining relationships. Networking needs to be done day after day, week after week, throughout your sales career. The more people you network with, the easier it is to find someone who can refer you to your target clients.

One way to expand your network quickly is to join groups. These can be alumni associations, affinity groups like the Italian American Association, trade associations, or groups whose sole purpose is to network. You also need to get involved -- volunteer to be on committees, join the board, any activity where you feel you can or want to be of help. The Optimal Salesperson participates in one or more such groups and engages with the members to connect with them as people. Thus they develop a strong foundation of resources.

Networking requires what we like to call an <u>abundance mentality</u>. Be more focused on giving than getting and you will receive even more in return. However, if you only concentrate on taking as much as you can from your contacts, you will soon wear out your welcome and relationships will deteriorate. If you are honestly interested in connecting and helping others in the network, your contact list will grow as rapidly as the people who are naturally attracted to you.

COLD CALL WHEN YOU NEED SALES NOW

Control of your destiny is essential to achieving goals. Introductions have a very high closing rate but it typically takes time to develop and grow a network of people. <u>Cold calling</u> is a direct route to the decision-makers and gives the salesperson control. But as mentioned earlier in this chapter, it has a low success rate compared to introductions.

However, if you start with a list, happen to correctly guess as to who is worried about a current problem, and have the skill to defeat the gatekeeper and get to the decision-makers, cold calling can provide a short cut to filling your pipeline and closing deals. However, if you don't know exactly who to reach, your hit rate will be low.

So, when cold calling, start at the top. The "top" is a relative term. For example, if you're selling a consulting service to small to medium-sized business, it probably means the owner or president. If you sell products to multinationals it's a different story. Here you might want to call the top person in the relevant department or unit. This person should have the authority, money, and willingness to fix the problem your product/service is designed to fix or have access to someone who can.

Yet "the top" is not always the person who experiences the problem. For example, if you sell copiers or document-imaging systems, the admin person may be struggling with an inadequate machine. Yet he or she rarely has the authority or the money to replace it. So you might want to call the department director or an operational vice-president. Since it is a cold call you probably don't know exactly who to talk to. So when finding this out, aim high. It is easier to be referred down than up. And never call and ask, "Who handles the purchase of copy machines?" You will likely be shunted down the chain of command and over to a purchasing agent who at best will get you involved in a bid process.

A few last words of advice on cold calling. Make a commitment or "trap" yourself into ensuring that you will do the cold calling necessary to meet your goals. It is never a crisis to make a cold call and plans to prospect can and often are derailed by an urgent client request or other fires that need to be put out. So tell someone important (boss, spouse, etc.) that your goal is to make "X" number of calls per week. Have them ask you how you did on Friday. Also, you should make an appointment with yourself to prospect. Put it in the calendar and treat it the same way as a regular appointment. Make it the first task of the day so you will tackle it right away.

USE MARKETING AS A BONUS

Leads provided by an effective marketing campaign are only a small part of prospecting. Marketing is the gravy to the "meat" of prospecting.

Consider the nature of marketing itself. You can drop 5,000 pieces of mail this week and get 50 leads. Drop the same piece next month, and you might get five. The response to marketing can depend on a wide variety of factors, from the weather, to the economy, even the mood of the President and Congress. You have even less control over marketing and advertising than cold calling.

8

Adopt and Use an Effective Selling Process

Process is an essential element of every successful professional. Engineers have a process they go through when they embark on a design project. Whether it is a two-story house or a thirty-story commercial building, the process is essentially the same. Sometimes the order of the steps is different and sometimes certain steps have different emphasis based on local conditions. For example, builders in California are more concerned about earthquakes than those in Pennsylvania. Heart surgeons, artists, landscapers, plumbers, auto mechanics and hair dressers also have their own processes as well.

Unfortunately, salespeople – and the companies that employ them -- rarely follow a clear-cut, consistent process. They generally "wing it" and get into patterns (better described as a rut) where every sales call turns out to be a new adventure, with often unpredictable results.

DEFINING A SALES PROCESS

A sales process can be defined as a sequence of steps you must go through to take a proposal from a name on a list to a paying customer. As with other processes, the order of steps varies; sometimes there is more emphasis on one phase than another. However, the process should always be discernable to an outside observer.

An engineer uses the same process to design a home (a few days) and an office building (a year). Likewise, a professional salesperson will use the same process for a simple, one-call close sale as for a long cycle, complex sale lasting a year or more. The intricacy of executing each step of the process will vary but the steps should be the same for both.

THE BENEFITS OF USING AN EFFECTIVE SALES PROCESS

Using a sales process consistently is good, but using a sales process that has a proven successful track record is better. Follows are the attributes of an effective process.

Replication

Without a sales process, salespeople are prone to what we like to call "center fielder syndrome." Imagine a baseball player who is in a major slump. He hasn't gotten a hit in two weeks. Then one day the center fielder absent-mindedly steps on third base and immediately afterwards hits a home run. Now he starts to think stepping on third base had something to do his success. So he steps on third base every time until he discovers his new "lucky" batting glove.

Salespeople act in much the same way. They often have

no idea why a prospect bought their product. So they ascribe the success to a particular sales technique, continuing to use it until it "stops working." The problem is that neither the center fielder nor the salesperson understands the difference between correlation and causality. Neither stepping on third base nor the technique caused the results.

However, the salesperson can become more efficient by using a time-tested and proven sales process. They will understand which actions cause which results and can eliminate extraneous activities, statements, questions, and steps. A sales process meeting the criteria described in this chapter will allow the salesperson to replicate successful outcomes and abort fruitless leads early on and without wasting resources.

Growth

Isolating and eliminating weaknesses are key to <u>growth</u> and will be discussed in great detail in Parts IV and V. When a salesperson consistently applies an effective selling process, various weaknesses must be surmounted to spur growth. Below is a discussion of how the sales process helped Kristen overcome her money weakness.

Case Study: Kristen

Kristin is uncomfortable discussing money with prospects. Without the sales process and left to her own devices, Kristin adds prospects to her pipeline that ultimately will not buy because they have no money. Yet she continues to spend resources on these prospects, including proposals and demos.

Few prospects tell her outright they have no money. Sometimes they just stop responding or come up an excuse like upper management, the economy, changing internal conditions, thereby obscuring the true reason for the lost sale and wasted time. Kristin and her manager might conclude that it was her lack of closing skills or that she just needed to work harder and see more people. They fail to realize the actual problem lies in her discomfort in discussing money when qualifying prospects.

Then Kristin and her manager go to sales training and learn about a sales process in which money is discussed during the first call. And it soon becomes obvious where Kristen's problem lie: she is reluctant (if not downright afraid) to discuss money early on.

It is now up to Kristen (and her manager) to take specific steps to help her overcome this weakness. One method might be to take a one-page list of questions into the call that would provide her "prompts" and reassurance in asking about money. Or she and her manager could devise an indirect line of questioning that would lead naturally to the money discussions. She could also try the money discussion out with smaller, non-threatening prospects until she got comfortable. (Chapter 12 discusses overcoming money weaknesses in more detail.) Whichever method they come up with, two of the key ingredients to Kristin's growth are having a sales process and being held accountable for it.

Once she overcomes her money weakness, Kristen will stop wasting her efforts. Prospects without money will be quickly disqualified from her pipeline, she will have more time to find better prospects, and will therefore have a higher close rate on proposals.

Eventually she will sell more, earn more, and function at a higher level. The sales process will have resulted in true and lasting growth for Kristen.

Resource Allocation

Limited resources are a fact of life. While ineffective salespeople chase anyone and everyone with equal vigor, the Optimal Salesperson only spends time with qualified prospects; that is, prospects who meet the qualification criteria as defined by the particular sales process being used. The key concept here is that it is the prospect that has to qualify to do business with you, not the other way around.

The Optimal Salesperson, even one who represents a small company selling to a multinational behemoth, realizes that they bring value to the table, have only so much time to spend, and refuse to waste any of it no matter how big the carrot the prospect dangles in front of them. In simple sales situations (one or two decision-makers) and short cycle (one or two calls) selling, the Optimal Salesperson will only spend time with prospects that are closeable. In long cycle complex sales, decisions about where to spend time and effort are not so clear-cut.

Relationship maps are valuable in helping to decide where to spend time in a complex, long cycle sale. A <u>relationship map</u> is a schematic diagram of those involved in either making or influencing the buying decision, including both formal and informal relationships. An effective sales process will address not only how to uncover the true relationships of the players but will dictate an understanding of all of the steps the prospect must go through to make a decision.

Using a process that includes these elements will keep the Optimal Salesperson focused on the people who have problems that need solving and those who can move the sale toward a close. It avoids wasting valuable resources on people with no effect on the outcome of the sale.

ATTRIBUTES OF AN EFFECTIVE SELLING PROCESS

Although an effective selling process has many attributes, the following are the most important.

Simplicity

Engineering is a complex process. It takes years to get to the point where a person can perform engineering tasks unsupervised. However, engineering is relatively easy to do once you gain knowledge and experience. (Just ask an engineer. They will tell you how easy it was. It helps confirm how smart they are.)

Selling, on the other hand, is very simple, but it is not so easy to do. Unlike engineering which involves specific duties and can be accomplished undisturbed, sales can be complicated by self-limiting beliefs, hidden weaknesses, and gatekeepers. Also unlike engineers, salespeople do their work in public meetings, sometimes with active interference, and must make decisions on the fly with no time for reflection or calculation.

To be effective, selling processes must be simple to execute. Consider the fact that everyone buys things at one time or another. If buying/selling were as complex as some selling regimens purport it to be, nothing would ever get sold and we would have little if any economic activity.

Adaptability

Different prospects buy differently even when companies are in the same industry. A company's buying process is also time dependent. Some companies may buy more quickly at the end of the year than the beginning or the process may slow down or speed up as the procurement progresses, depending on changing conditions.

Many variables come into play when products and services are purchased. These include the size of the deal, importance of the product, time of the year, experience of the buyer, and countless others.

So, to be effective, a sales process must adapt to the situation at hand. An inflexible selling "system" that includes multiple steps which must be performed in a set order can put the salesperson in the position of trying to force his process on the prospect. At best, this makes the salesperson seem unresponsive and pushy and at worst, will cause the salesperson to totally miss opportunities or be excluded by the prospect.

Adaptability must also apply to the person doing the selling and the product or service being marketed. The personality of the salesperson must be compatible with the process so she appears natural and not "salesy" or forced to the prospect. Similarly, before you adopt a sales process, make sure it is well-matched with all the products and services you represent.

Applicability

Architects and other builders have a universally applicable process or set of procedures. Regardless of what they construct, whether it's a twenty-story building, a two-story house, or the Washington Monument, the process is applicable in every case. Although it is adaptable and applied differently to each situation, they work from the same basic principles using the same general process.

When you choose a sales process, make sure it is universally applicable. For example, if you offer both products and services, avoid a process that emphasizes hands-on demonstrations of features and benefits. Although you can show how software works, it is difficult to do a demo of timely and responsive customer service.

Prospect-Centered

Most salespeople approach the market using what we like to call "me-centered selling." They focus on themselves, their companies, and their product. Even when using need-based or solution selling methodologies, they still spend most of the time talking about themselves or their products. When these me-centered salespeople are supposedly in the discovery phase of the process, they are really thinking about how they can make their products fit the need or problem being discussed. They spend their discovery time waiting for a chance to pounce on the prospect with their sales presentation.

The paradox is that the more time you spend totally focused on the prospect with a mindset of truly trying to understand whether they qualify to do business with you, the more control you have over the sales process. Thus the less you think about your product or service on a sales call, the more of it you will sell because you are concentrating on whether your product or service truly fits their needs.

This cannot be faked. The Optimal Salesperson comes across as authentic and believable precisely because they have a sincere interest in the prospect's situation and are willing to say when they can't help. The Optimal Salesperson never appears like they are selling; ironically this makes them more effective than if they spent the time in me-centered activities like pitching, presenting, and providing demonstrations.

Oriented Toward Buying Motivation

Excited prospects can be the most dangerous. They appear so ramped up about your product that you may be tempted to abandon the selling process, skip the qualifying part, and just close the deal. Another pitfall is to mistake apparent interest in your product or service with a bona fide need or with an actual intent to buy.

The Optimal Salesperson employs a sales process that emphasizes buying motivation. Some selling regimes call it pain; others talk about urgency or a compelling reason to buy. Regardless, a major component is a discovery phase with the motivation to buy as its centerpiece. Buying motivation needs to be a critical part of your selling process; otherwise you'll waste time with "interested" and "excited" prospects who never purchase anything.

Additional Factors

Unsuccessful salespeople are very <u>predictable</u>. Say the phone rings, you answer it, and can immediately tell from the canned pitch that it is a salesperson. If you are like most people, you begin to figure out how to get rid of the caller. Many salespeople adopt processes and techniques similar to everyone else, thus making them eminently defeatable. Prospects see them coming a mile away and immediately take steps to extricate themselves from the encounter.

Whichever sales process you subscribe to, you must adapt it to your personality and your products and apply it to your unique situation. If you are <u>authentic</u>, you will come across as "natural" and not "canned" and have a better chance of connecting with the prospect. For the Optimal Salesperson, the sales call is a real interpersonal interaction and not a series of easily transparent moves, techniques, and steps.

<u>Personality</u> is less important to success in sales than most people think. The general belief is that to be in sales you must be outgoing and a "people person." However, personality is not even listed in the attributes of the Optimal Salesperson discussed in Chapter 3. In fact, two of the most effective and highly developed salespeople we know prefer to be left alone. They can be personable when necessary, but rarely seek out human contact unless they are selling.

We have also worked with many ineffective people who have the typical "sales personality." They lacked focus, persistence, and other qualities necessary for a successful sales career.

Personality can have an impact on how you employ sales techniques, engage with people, or deliver a message. But whether you are outgoing or reserved, dominant or cooperative, amiable or expressive, you can be effective in sales if you have motivation, a supportive belief system and use an effective selling process.

Finally sales processes should be <u>transferable</u> to many industries. What happens if you change jobs or switch areas of concentration? Industry-specific sales processes tend to be more rigid and less flexible, making it harder to adapt to change. The Optimal Salesperson builds a career based on a sales process grounded in universally applicable principles that can be adapted on a continual basis depending on the situation.

DEVELOPING AND ADAPTING A SELLING PROCESS

So which sales process should you choose? Dozens of books can provide advice and guidance. It goes without saying that you should use a process that is already documented, tested, and proven successful as well as meeting all the criteria laid out in this chapter. We recommend BASELINE SELLING by David Kurlan, which applies to just about every type of sales endeavor.

Since any process will require some adaptation, engage a sales coach to help you achieve your ultimate potential. This coach should not only be well-versed in the fine points of sales, but also understand the relationship of belief systems to performance and have experience helping salespeople overcoming hidden weaknesses. The coach should provide you with feedback, observing what you say and do and offering insight as to how you can be more effective.

The Optimal Salesperson also needs to be self-aware and observant when adapting a sales process. Be conscious of what you are doing, saying, and feeling and notice the results and responses you get. This will help you adjust your approach week-to-week, day-to-day, even minute-to-minute within the same sales call. If you start with a proven sales process and apply the principles, observe and adjust continually; in a few months it should be fine-tuned to meet your needs. You can then focus more energy on overcoming self-limiting beliefs and hidden weaknesses as well as strengthening your overall sales ability.

9

Practice and Internalize
Interpersonal Selling Skills

The secret to accomplishing any task is first, knowing how to do it and second, having the right tools. In sales, the "task" is to close the sale which entails advancing the prospect through the gates of the selling process. The "tools" the salesperson uses are interpersonal skills that include several abilities -- quickly developing bonding and rapport, asking questions effectively, qualifying a prospect, and closing, among others.

DEFINING INTERPERSONAL SKILLS

Most sales trainers and many sales managers view interpersonal skills as a collection of tips, tricks, and techniques to be used on the prospect. However, we believe that they are more complex yet fundamental. We define interpersonal skill as an ability to communicate with people in a certain way to accomplish a certain task. This ability has many facets; and in many ways is as complex as painting a picture, which requires equal parts imagination, perception, and a deft touch with a brush, among other things. Thus the skill of prospecting, for example, will include the abilities to quickly get and hold a prospect's attention; to understand if the prospect has a problem you can help with, along with the willingness to pick up the phone in the first place. The Optimal Salesperson possesses many interpersonal skills and constantly seeks to add new skills and improve the ones he has.

LISTENING – THE MOST IMPORTANT SKILL

<u>Listening</u> is without a doubt the most important skill a salesperson can possess. So many authors have expounded at great length on this subject that emphasizing it seems almost like a cliché. Yet our day-to-day work with salespeople reveals that most of them just don't listen to prospects. As mentioned in Chapter 8, they have a me-centered selling process that predisposes them to talk instead of listen. And when they think they are "listening" what they are really doing is waiting for a break in the prospect's stream of words so that they can begin talking again.

Effective listening begins with the mindset that what the prospect says is actually more important that what you say… both to you and the prospect. Once that belief is in place, effective listening becomes very easy.

The four aspects of good listening are hearing, decoding, inferring, and verifying. <u>Hearing</u> involves focusing on the actual words the prospect is saying without thinking about yourself and what you want to say. <u>Decoding</u> entails extracting meaning from the words from the perspective of the prospect. Words and phrases may have different meanings for prospect than the salesperson. <u>Inferring</u> is necessary because most people leave much of what they are trying to communicate unsaid. The assumption is that the listener is looking at the situation from the speaker's perspective and can fill in the blanks.

Inferring is a highly developed skill. An empathic listener, having decoded what was said, will infer meaning behind what was actually spoken. This ability is enhanced by knowledge of the product, the industry, and the prospect's business. Thus, with experience, a salesperson can become a better listener.

Finally, a good listener will confirm what she thinks she heard by <u>verifying</u> it with the prospect. An example of verification might sound like, "Joe, to be clear, I heard you say that your current machine is hurting performance. Did you mean that it is solely responsible for reduced production or just a contributing factor?" An Optimal Salesperson who excels at all four aspects of listening reduces misunderstandings to a minimum and enhances all other interpersonal skills.

BONDING AND RAPPORT – THE CONDUIT FOR INFORMATION

Flow of information from the prospect to the salesperson is the primary goal of an effective sales call. The relationship with the prospect is the conduit over that this information flows. The ability to quickly develop a relationship or bond with the prospect will enhance one's ability to get prospects to share more, deeper, and richer information and even emotional content. This ability will allow you to more effectively move the prospect through the gates of your selling process.

There are three distinct phrases to developing a bond: interaction, engagement, and connection. Almost every salesperson has the ability to interact with people. <u>Interaction</u> just means you say something and they respond.

For example:

> Salesperson: "I notice you went to Villanova."
>
> Prospect: "Yes."
>
> Salesperson: "When did you graduate?"
>
> Prospect: "1985."

The second phrase, <u>engagement</u>, means that you have succeeded in getting the prospect "involved" in a conversation. They ask questions, you ask questions, they provide input as do you. Continuing the example:

> Salesperson: "Were you there when they won the NCAA Basketball Championship?"
>
> Prospect: "Yeah! I had season tickets. It was an exciting time. Did you go to school there?"
>
> Salesperson: "1965-69."
>
> Prospect: "What was your major?"
>
> Salesperson: "Engineering. What was yours?"
>
> Prospect: "Business."

Notice how the prospect became engaged in the conversation, picking up the thread and moving it forward.

<u>Connection</u> happens when the discussion leads to a bond between the two people. Anything can create the bond: a shared experience, a common memory, or a mutual friend. Connections can also happen during a business meeting when the salesperson asks enough good questions or makes statements that demonstrate that he "gets it." The salesperson and prospect are then on the same page and a bond has been developed. Every salesperson has experienced this at one time or another because it is the same process by which two people

become friends. Although social friendship is not the goal here, the process is the same.

QUALIFYING PROSPECTS – ONE KEY TO EFFICIENT SELLING

Buyers do not want to be "sold," but would rather feel like they are in control of the sales process. However, they understand that the salesperson is usually eager to demonstrate that their product or service will solve the problem at hand and is superior to the competition.

The average salesperson is "leaning forward" and thus becomes easy prey for the prospect. Salespeople who are too eager to write proposals end up wasting lots of time with unqualified prospects. The Optimal Salesperson does not lean forward but instead thinks through which prospects she should bid, quote, or propose. The Optimal Salesperson only writes proposals for worthy prospects.

So who is worthy of receiving a proposal? The definition of a qualified prospect will vary, depending on the sales process being used. To qualify to get a proposal, the prospect should, at a minimum, be willing to do the following:

- Share their true buying motivations.

- Describe the complete decision-making process.

- Have a discussion about how much they are willing to spend and be willing to pay for "value."

- Agree to make a decision upon delivery of the quote. (This decision may be delayed if multiple people and complex decision processes are involved.)

The Optimal Salesperson is efficient and only writes the proposal after the prospect proves to be worthy and qualified.

ASKING GOOD QUESTIONS – ANOTHER KEY TO EFFICIENT SELLING

<u>Intellectual questions</u> are the easiest to ask and pose no threat to the prospect or to the salesperson. These are the type of questions that, when answered, provide the basic data you need to understand the nature of the project and prepare the proposal. Intellectual questions generally yield data about how big, how many, how often, how much, what time, when, and so on.

Unfortunately, many salespeople restrict their questioning to the intellectual level and never ask a <u>tough question</u>, one that involves some level of risk. Salespeople are often afraid that prospects may not answer tough questions -- they may feel it's too intrusive or possibly even offensive. However, the level of "risk" is perceived through the lens of one's own self-limiting belief systems. As belief systems are eliminated, the amount of risk is seen as diminishing and the questions seem easier to ask. The Optimal Salesperson, having overcome most, if not all self-limiting beliefs, sees no risk at all and is willing to ask any and all questions.

Case Study: Mark

Mark's sales were depressed because he wasted a lot of time with unqualified prospects. He got all the basic data about a project, but consistently failed to uncover two key pieces of information -- he never knew the client's true motivation and never found out how much money the prospect wanted to spend.

Co-author Marie started to debrief his sales calls, uncovering the fact that he was afraid to ask questions about the client's motivation and budget, feeling they were either none of his business or dealt with information the client guarded closely. Marie realized that these beliefs were hampering Mark's ability to execute the sales process because he wouldn't ask what he perceived to be tough questions. However, after three months of extensive coaching using the principles in Part IV, Mark was able to alter his mindset. The questions no longer seemed threatening so he just asked. No special techniques were required.

DISCUSSING MONEY – A RARE SKILL

We've said this before: Excited prospects can dangerous. We always get worried when salespeople report that "the prospect loved our presentation" because we know what's coming next.

More often than not, when asked if the prospect has any money the salesperson's reply is "we didn't get to it" or "I forgot to ask" or "Money won't be a problem, they have plenty of money and they were really excited about what we could do for them."

The hidden weaknesses that cause salespeople to avoid discussing money are explored in depth in Chapter 12. For purposes here, it is only important to understand that discussing money is a skill of vital importance to the Optimal Salesperson. Discussing money sets you apart from your competitors, 65 percent of whom are uncomfortable doing so.

If what you sell costs more than the competitor's version, it is imperative to discuss money, and to let the prospect know you are more expensive. This is the only way you can find out whether the prospect values your advantages enough to pay extra for them. The Optimal Salesperson spends whatever time and energy it takes to master this critical skill.

CALLING AT THE APPROPRIATE LEVEL

Being referred down the chain of command within an organization is much easier than working your way up the organization chart. Calling at the top does not always mean the CEO. It could be the VP of operations (as opposed to the project manager) the chief financial officer (not the accounts payable manager). The rule of thumb is to call the person who owns the biggest problem that your product or service will solve. Bigger problems exist – and bigger decisions are made -- at the top of the organization. If you are not comfortable calling there, then see Chapter 18 to help overcome the hidden weaknesses related to this skill.

Dealing with Technical Experts

Another challenge salespeople face is dealing with technical experts, both theirs and the client's. Technical experts scare many salespeople. This is understandable; most salespeople must rely on others in their organization to help with technical information. But that doesn't mean the salesperson should take the technical expert on every sales call and turn them loose on prospects and watch the fireworks like the shootout at the OK Corral. In many cases the decision-makers in the prospect organization don't understand their own experts either but depend on them to make sure that whatever they are buying is compatible with their in-house technology and processes.

The technical issues should be viewed as just one hurdle to clear before the sale is complete. Treat the client's technical expert like any other person who needs to be sold and use your selling process on them. Concentrate on their concerns and what they care about. Then, if a meeting with your company's technical expert is required, direct him or her to delve into only those details that matter to the prospect. The Optimal

Salesperson controls the sales process end-to-end and knows how to deal with all types of people in both their and the prospect's organization.

CONFRONTING A PROSPECT

Confrontation is always a controversial topic in sales. In all of our years of dealing with salespeople we have never had anyone ask us to teach them how to be confrontational. However, sometimes it's unavoidable.

Yet the issue is usually not confrontation between salesperson and prospect. It is getting the prospect to confront the real problem or the facts of the situation. Many times in meetings with owners and CEOs, the authors have difficulty getting the CEO to realize that the sales force is stagnant; that their "best" salesperson lacks the skills to take them to the next level; or that the sales manager who has been with the company ten years needs to learn how to effectively grow the sales force. Obviously this is unhappy news for the CEO. But topics like these are inevitable in the selling process. The CEO must be approached directly and respectfully but firmly. Problem areas, no matter how sensitive or emotion-laden, must be addressed. You may need to use confrontation to help clients achieve clarity and progress through the sales process.

Fear usually prevents a salesperson from getting the prospect to confront the real problem: fear that they won't be liked; that the prospect will be angry; that they will lose the project or perhaps even worse, credibility; or that the prospect will take a question as a personal attack. The Optimal Salesperson knows that credibility is enhanced when real problems are uncovered and confronted and that real progress in the selling process can only begin when that happens.

Prospects have plenty of people willing to tell them what they want to hear and respect those who can say "the emperor he has no clothes." The Optimal Salesperson realizes that having respect is more imperative than being liked. And most importantly, the Optimal Salesperson has the interpersonal skills to present the truth gently and in a nurturing way so that if won't be seen as a personal attack.

DEALING WITH EMOTIONS

<u>Pushing a person's buttons</u> is terminology psychologists use to describe a process where one person picks the exact thing to say or to do that elicits an emotional response from the person they are interacting with. You've experienced the phenomenon if you've ever made an innocent comment and gotten an unexpected and passion-filled response from a friend or relative. Most likely you have inadvertently said or done something that reminded the other person of someone else and they reacted to that someone…you just happened to be there.

The Optimal Salesperson is aware of this process and remains in control of their emotions. Sometimes you ask a question and the prospect reacts emotionally, by either getting excited or angry. The Optimal Salesperson remains dispassionate, while seeking to understand what is going on.

If the prospect is excited, they will continue to follow their sales process; they may remind the prospect that the solution will cost more than originally planned or that it still has to be tested for the proposed application. If the prospect is angry, the Optimal Salesperson will not take it personally and will stay "in the moment" and ask why the prospect is feeling upset.

Most importantly, the Optimal Salesperson is aware of his own "buttons" and knows how not to react when they are pushed by the prospect. You must be conscious of who the prospect is and why you are there, keeping yourself and your own issues out of play. Chapter 13 discusses how to stay in the moment in more detail.

CLOSING – GETTING TO "NO"

Closing is generally misunderstood. The general belief is that closing is a dramatic event that happens at the end of a long battle with the prospect. Movies like "Glengarry Glen Ross" popularize that notion. In reality, closing is merely a natural consequence of all that went before.

For example, say we told you that we would set you up with five appointments next week. All had a serious problem with serious consequences that you could fix; they had enough money to fix the problem; they had authority to make a decision; and had agreed to make a decision based on what you had to tell them. How many could you close? Most people say all five. The most conservative might say three out of the five.

Now imagine that the definition of closing is to get either a "Yes" or a "No." The answer would be definitely five. The important point here is that you gave your answer without knowing what was going to be said at the meeting next week. So it is not the closing itself that is important but rather the all that goes before that is most critical.

The Optimal Salesperson knows that opening is the critical skill. <u>Opening</u> is the process of getting the prospect qualified and to the point of making a decision. If that is done properly, anyone can close.

Most definitions of closing imply that it means getting a "Yes." But perhaps a better definition might be, "Closing is the process of guiding the prospect to the point where they can say 'Yes' or 'No.'" Sometimes the "No" comes very early in the process and that can be a good thing.

Salespeople dislike "No" but it can be the second best word they hear. It lets you know where you stand; the sooner you can get to it in the process, the faster you can move onto something else. Keeping prospects in the pipeline when the ultimate answer is going to be "No" reduces the accuracy of forecasts.

The Optimal Salesperson seeks to get a "No" as soon as the prospect has decided effectively that the competition has won the deal. Many times this is months before the formal announcement, Frequently the Optimal Salesperson knows the answer will be "No" before the prospect is willing to admit it.

Conserving resources is vitally important. The Optimal Salesperson realizes that selling resources such as technical help, emotional energy, face time with prospects, and so on, are limited and should be applied only to high value targets. Wasting them on low probability prospects leads to frustration, reluctance of support staff to help on future projects, and ultimately to lower income.

Walking away from prospects when there is still a mathematical chance, however small, to win is one of the more difficult things for salespeople to do, particularly when the pipeline is weak. But failure to do so is one of the reasons pipelines are weak. The Optimal Salesperson knows that walking away from dying but not yet dead deals provides the time to prospect for the high probability ones. Paradoxically, getting more "Nos" is one of the fastest ways to pump up the pipeline with more prospects who will ultimately say "Yes."

PART IV

IDENTIFYING AND OVERCOMING HIDDEN OBSTACLES TO SALES EFFECTIVENESS

THE OPTIMAL SALESPERSON

10

The General Process for Dealing with Hidden Obstacles

Hidden weaknesses are a lot like the wind. You can't see wind directly. However, if you see leaves turning, branches bending, and trees swaying, you can deduce that the wind must be blowing. Likewise, we can observe actions salespeople take and the results will betray the existence of their hidden obstacles. <u>Hidden obstacles</u> are deeply held beliefs, attributes, and needs not detectable by direct observation but rather only by their effects.

The origin of hidden weaknesses is both unimportant and difficult to determine. It does not really matter why, for example, you are uncomfortable discussing money. It would take months if not years of psychoanalysis to uncover the root cause of this fear and other obstacles. In truth, most self-limiting beliefs are programmed in by teachers, bosses, society, coaches and even parents; all with positive intent and most often for good reason and without understanding the consequences.

DISCOVERING HIDDEN OBSTACLES

Behavior results from beliefs. By <u>behavior</u> we mean sales activity such as number of sales calls, number of appointments, and so on. Behavior also means how we act on sales calls which includes what we say, how we say it, and who we say it to. It also includes how we react to what others say.

An easy way to discover hidden weaknesses is with an evaluation designed specifically to detect them. The website www.caramanico.com will give you more information about one such evaluation. Another way is to carefully observe what you do and how you act and compare that to an objective standard. That is why having a sales process and a well-developed set of interpersonal skills are so important. A sales coach or mentor is also important, since it is difficult to evaluate and hold yourself accountable to the standard. An objective and knowledgeable third party can identify shortcomings and suggest a course of corrective action.

ELIMINATING HIDDEN OBSTACLES

Quantum leaps forward in sales effectiveness happen when you eliminate hidden weaknesses. For example, if you had need for approval and got rid of it, your sales effectiveness would increase by about 50 percent. However, this type of change can be quite difficult.

Figure 10.1 illustrates the growth curve for the typical salesperson who is actively working on improving. Incremental growth happens as the salesperson learns and internalizes new sales processes and interpersonal skills. As soon as a hidden weakness or self-limiting belief is overcome, there is a jump in effectiveness that is characterized by a noticeable jump in outcomes. Hard questions are suddenly no problem to ask, prospects share their budget, or referrals start to flow in, all because a hidden weakness disappeared. As you can see from the illustration, the transition is somewhat jagged, what mathematicians call a discontinuity in the growth curve.

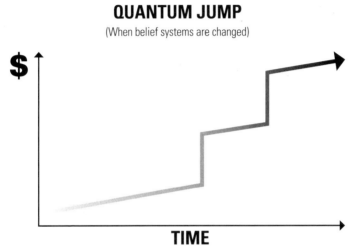

QUANTUM JUMP
(When belief systems are changed)

TIME

Figure 10.1. Quantum Jump.

Hidden weaknesses do not go away easily; getting rid of them requires persistence and expenditure of emotional energy. Anyone was has ever tried to overcome a fear of rejection or tried to get comfortable about money can attest to that. However, you must first decide you want to change the belief. The decision must then be followed by action and persistence.

Self-limiting beliefs tend to go away all at once. You either have a belief or you don't. It's like Santa Claus. One day a seven-year-old believes in Santa Claus wholeheartedly. The next day he doesn't. The child may have a brief period of doubt, but it is usually very short.

Beliefs are brittle, like glass shelves. If you overload a wooden shelf with books, it will sag giving you a warning that it is about to collapse. But a glass shelf looks the same until the second it collapses into a pile of shards and books on the floor. You get no advance notice. Like glass shelves, self-limiting beliefs are strong up until the very day they disappear. Just as the length of time it takes for the glass shelf to fail depends on the how long it takes to pile up enough books and how thick the glass is, so the length of time it takes to overcome a self-limiting belief depends on how much energy you put into changing the belief and how deeply held that belief is. It can vary from a month or two to as long as a year or two.

Salespeople often make the common mistake of deciding to change without taking any action. This renders the "decision" academic because nothing ever happens. Another mistake is trying to fix everything at once. Choose one hidden weakness at a time and work on it. When that is conquered, you can then move on to another.

EIGHT STEPS TO OVERCOMING HIDDEN BELIEFS

What follows is an eight-step process for overcoming self-limiting beliefs and hidden weaknesses.

Step 1 - Choose One to Work on

Choosing is simple; pick the belief that is causing you the most trouble today. So how do you tell which one is affecting you the most? Be aware of what you are doing and feeling before, during, and after sales calls and become a keen observer of the outcomes these actions (or inactions) and feelings produce. You will soon notice repetitive patterns and what you need to work on will become obvious.

Case Study: Liz

Liz was modestly successful but unhappy with her income. We evaluated her and found several beliefs and weaknesses that needed to change. As she started to adopt her new sales process she debriefed herself each day and after most of her sales interactions.

Initially, she had disagreed with the evaluation's findings of a need for approval. But after three weeks she began to notice that she found plenty of excuses not to prospect, shied away from asking tough qualifying questions, and was reluctant to close when the opportunity was there. She also became aware of not taking risks on sales calls. Being honest with herself, she realized that she was looking for their approval. Once she confronted reality, the situation was obvious and the choice was easy.

Step 2 - Enumerate How It Affects You

Money is the first thing salespeople think of when they consider the ramifications of hidden weakness. Admittedly, not making enough money is a major motivator for change and is also one of the major results of hidden weaknesses. But there are other results as well. Low close rates that cause long work hours can deprive your family of your time and energy. There is nothing worse that missing your child's school event because you had to work on a proposal that you have no chance of winning. Another powerful motivator for change is loss of self-respect. When you finally become aware of what holding onto a self-limiting belief is costing in terms of effectiveness, you start to realize that you are worth more than what you are getting from your selling career. And it is hard to respect someone, even yourself, who is underperforming. Loss of self-respect is one of the more powerful growth motivators and provides a great impetus for change.

Step 3 - Commit to Changing

Deciding to change is the first step to commitment to change; but it is far from enough. Commitment to change and growth means that you will do whatever it takes to get there. You will suffer (perceived) indignity, risk failure, actually fail, be rejected, be uncomfortable, brave the unknown, try new things, adjust your approach, and never give up until the new empowering belief is internalized or the hidden weakness overcome. One way to do this is to identify in advance what you are willing to give up, what you are willing to risk, and what outcomes you will suffer through to achieve the desired state. Most people discover that what actually happens is not half as bad as they think will happen. If you are willing to accept what you think will happen, the rest will fall into place.

One method to ensure that your commitment sticks is to paint yourself into a figurative corner. Tell your spouse or boss what you are going to do. You won't want to let them down. Or put an appointment on your calendar to prospect, then bring a new salesperson in your office to watch how you do it as a learning exercise, ostensibly for them. You will discover courage you did not know you had and your colleague may actually learn something.

Step 4 - Adopt the Proper Mindset

Before beginning the change process, you must identify the proper mindset. You know what your belief is now or you wouldn't have decided to change it. Let's assume you want to get better at getting referrals but don't believe people will give them to you. You must realize that this belief needs to change if you are ever to become effective at getting referrals.

There are two ways to approach this. First, you could adopt the opposite belief to the one you currently have. In this case, you would consciously seek to adopt the following belief: "Clients will give me referrals." It will help to give some reasons for the new belief such as, "I have helped them many times." "People generally want to help." "I give referrals, why shouldn't they?"

The second way to approach the problem is to find someone who excels at getting referred and adopt that person's belief. This works especially well because the belief has some validity since you know at least one person who got great results. In this case, you would find a person successful at getting referrals and ask them what they are thinking and doing when they ask for a referral.

Step 5 – Identify the Winning Behavior

Successful salespeople are often good role models for winning behavior (level of sales activity, the work ethic, methods of prospecting, sales process, techniques, demeanor, and so on). However, be careful to separate out idiosyncratic behavior from solid winning behavior. For example, co-author Dan worked with a salesperson who swore the key to success was always getting his car washed and his shoes shined before every sales call. This may have had a minor effect but it was hardly the main reason for his success.

When you observe a successful salesperson doing certain things it's always a good idea to ask him why he is doing them.

This will help you to establish a cause and effect and identify the exact behaviors that lead to a winning sales career. Another good source of winning behaviors is the sales manager. They should have a wealth of knowledge and experience and can describe what behaviors lead to success. However, not all sales managers are created equal – some can actually be the cause of problems in the sales department. But a successful sales manager can be an invaluable resource of guidance and advice.

Many times, the winning behavior is obvious. For example, to get more referrals you need to ask for them more often. To get better qualified prospects, you may need to ask all prospects what their decision process is, and to avoid overpricing, you need to discuss money on the first sales call. No matter how you do it, you must define what constitutes a winning behavior.

Step 6 – Reinforce the Mindset Daily

Affirmations are a time-tested and proven method to condition your mindset on a daily basis. Affirmations are short, positively worded statements that you repeat daily or hourly to change your belief or attitude about yourself. Typically, you write them down on a note card and read them regularly and frequently.

The idea behind affirmations is that if you say it often enough, you will at some point start to actually believe it. Some examples of affirmations are: "People want to give me referrals." "I can sell large accounts." "I am a winner." and so on.

Another excellent way to reinforce your new mindset is to make an audio CD and play it in your car, computer, or iPod. Hearing the affirmation in your own voice somehow seems to have a greater effect than hearing some generic voice tell you the same thing.

Still another way to reinforce the mindset regularly is to put up signs in your office that remind you of the belief you are trying to adopt. Football coaches use this with great effect, posting attitudes they want the team to adopt on the team bulletin board.

However you do it, one thing is certain: The belief won't change on its own. You have to work at it and the more input you have to your subconscious, the faster the belief will change.

Step 7 – Act "As If" at All Times

You've now identified the proper mindset, you've determined the appropriate behavior, now you need to adapt the behavior you identified and act "as if" you had the proper belief. At first your attempts will be weak since you don't actually have the right belief so you are merely going through the motions. You probably won't get the outcome you were hoping for at first, but the outcome will probably be different than what you have been getting.

Case Study: Darrin

Darrin was trying to upgrade his client base by calling on CEOs instead of project managers and engineers. He determined that he needed to upgrade his wardrobe and start believing that he belonged in the "C" suite instead of down on the second floor with the project people.

So Darrin bought some new clothes and started the mindset conditioning described in Step 6. It took about four months and 20 meetings with CEOs before he finally felt comfortable and calling at the top was no longer an issue.

However, in the beginning, he took a lot of grief from his colleagues. They teased him about his new clothes. They asked who he thought he was, since only company executives called at the top. Everyone knew calling CEOs was a waste of time since the real decisions were made at the engineering level.

Nevertheless, Darrin persevered through both the external criticism and his own self-doubt. Results were poor at first but finally the new belief kicked in and he began to feel more comfortable in front of the executives. Things were easier up there – more relaxed but more focused. In his sixth month he closed a very big deal and became the envy of the rest of the sales team. They were unaware of the emotional work that Darrin has put in and when they found out about Darrin's success an amusing thing happened. They began to wear better clothes and talk about calling at the top, although few if any actually adopted Darrin's behavior.

Step 8 – Hold Yourself Accountable

Be honest with yourself. Pay attention to what you do and say and what feelings come up when you are doing it and saying it; or preparing to do it or say it. No one knows better than you when you are getting in your own way. This is especially true once you have become aware of your possible problems.

Review your sales activity against your plan. Did you do what you were supposed to do? Debrief yourself about your sales process. Did you follow it? Did you use interpersonal sales skills? Notice where you fell short.

Whatever you do, own your problem areas. Don't make excuses but don't get down on yourself. Don't get depressed because you didn't fix the problem after three tries. You will fail many times before you conquer the obstacle. Just remember that the monetary and psychic rewards of overcoming the hidden obstacle will be worth the effort.

If you have trouble holding yourself accountable, get someone you trust to do it for you. Tell them not to let you off the hook. Spouses, sales managers, and sales coaches are good resources. Just share with them what you are working on and report actions and outcomes to them regularly. This will speed up the process significantly.

EMOTIONAL INVESTMENTS PAY OFF

The Optimal Salesperson is persistent. <u>Persistence</u> means staying in the game and not giving up if first, second and even 35th attempts fail. Persistence means fighting your own instincts when you know they are wrong. Persistence means acting counter to your own beliefs when you know they are holding you back.

Effecting change requires both internal and external persistence. Most salespeople know how to persist externally by making repeated calls to the decision-maker until they get through, for instance. But persistence also needs to be directed internally in much the same way to eliminate self-limiting beliefs. When emotional energy is persistently applied over a period of time, self-limiting beliefs will give way to new, empowering beliefs that will in turn lead to tremendous growth in both your personal satisfaction and bank account.

THE OPTIMAL SALESPERSON

11

Eliminating the Need for Approval

Need for approval has wide-ranging effects on the effectiveness of a salesperson. Conquer it and your effectiveness will increase by about 50 - 60 percent.

WHAT IS THE NEED FOR APPROVAL?

Needing the approval of others is a human condition. We all require human contact and want to know that we are accepted. It becomes an issue when we seek it in the wrong places. The appropriate place to get approval is from parents, spouses, mentors, ministers, and priests, rabbis, and sales managers. However, a salesperson who seeks approval from prospects becomes very vulnerable. Needy salespeople are at the mercy of prospects who can control the sales process by manipulating them through granting or withholding approval. Actually, prospects do not have to do anything, as salespeople seeking approval will twist themselves into a pretzel in an effort to gain approval from the prospect.

From prospecting to closing, the effects of need for approval are pervasive. This hidden obstacle to sales affects more parts of the sales process than any other. A salesperson who has need for approval will not execute any sales technique which he perceives to be aggressive. It becomes more important to the salesperson that the prospects like him than that they do business with him. Strange as it sounds, the salesperson would rather have the prospects' approval than their money. Salespeople deny this, of course. And it is easy to pretend that it doesn't exist because the process is subconscious. The salesperson is unaware how his and the prospects' actions and words result from the salesperson's need for approval.

Need for approval is insidious because it combines with other self-limiting beliefs to hide itself. If salespeople believe they must call on purchasing agents first, they will perceive a suggestion from the sales manager or trainer to call on the operations vice-president as aggressive. Such activities violate their need for approval although they will couch it as a disagreement of philosophy.

Truck drivers, accountants, authors, auto mechanics, and window washers can have need for approval with no effect on either their job performance or their income. But it is an issue in the sales profession. And people with need for approval tend to end up in sales because there is plenty of opportunity to get approval they so desperately seek, although most are reluctant to admit it. If you are thinking it's not a problem for you, take a closer look at how you interact with prospects.

SYMPTOMS OF NEED FOR APPROVAL

Avoidance is one way to spot excess need for approval. The Optimal Salesperson may not like either making cold calls or asking for referrals but she doesn't avoid them. Few people enjoy being rejected 15 times per day, it is a necessary part of building a new territory. The Optimal Salesperson also realizes that it is not the salesperson the prospect is rejecting, only the product or service. She gets acceptance where she needs it -- at home and from her sales manager.

Avoiding any type of situation where the potential for conflict exists is a sure sign of need for approval. However, do not make the determination based on social interactions but only on sales or business interactions. Dodging a confrontation with your neighbor about his tree hanging over your fence will not hurt your sales effectiveness. Not prospecting regularly, failing to collect an overdue invoice, and avoiding the right questions or calling at the right level will have a major effect on your income.

Acceptance is another easy way to spot need for approval. The salesperson with need for approval accepts everything the prospect says without comment or question. When the prospect says they need it delivered by January 20th, they write it down but do not ask why. If the prospect says they need a consultant with a background in metallurgy and social work, a need for approval will cause you to write it down but not ask why that strange combination of skills is important to the success of the project. A person with strong need for approval will not be able to push back. They would be uncomfortable saying to the prospect, "January 20th could be a little hard to make. Is there a reason that date is important?"

Reluctance to ask probing questions is another symptom of need for approval. Salespeople see such questions as risky, aimed at getting information that prospects view as sensitive, proprietary, or personal. The weak salesperson will weigh the risk of asking such questions to be greater than the benefit any answers might bring. Also, when the prospect provides information that seems to conflict with what the salesperson's knows, strong need for approval prevents the salesperson from asking about it. For example, if a Sales managers find this maddening because a question that seemed so obvious was not addressed. When the reason was, "it didn't seem like the right time, " then need for approval is usually the culprit.

Need for approval can also result in excessive <u>proposal writing and quote preparation</u>, two tasks that frequently occupy the biggest block of time in a salesperson's schedule. When close rates are high and the proposals lead to a sale, that is a good thing. But it's a red flag when close rates are low and proposals and quotes are being written for unqualified prospects who rarely buy. Although unqualified quotes could mean a bad buy cycle, an ineffective sales process or a skills issue, it also might also indicate the need for approval. Need for approval can prevent the salesperson from asking the probing questions necessary to qualify the prospect or tell the prospect that they are not at the proposal point yet. It could also just be a convenient way to avoid prospecting which itself indicates need for approval.

MR. APPROVAL: JAUNTY JERRY

Jerry was a confident individual and when he learned about the effects of having a need for approval at an introductory seminar, he was glad he didn't have to worry about that. Jerry had an MBA from a prestigious college and had made a name for himself as a good businessperson, rising rapidly through the ranks to vice-president of a large professional services firm. Success followed success with no setbacks over a fourteen-year corporate career. So it was with a good self-image and a fat Rolodex that Jerry began his second career as an independent consultant.

One year later he was back in our office. He survived that first year...barely. Jerry remembered the seminar and came to us sheepishly admitting that, "I think I have more need for approval than I thought. It's holding me back. Can you help?"

Prospecting was never a priority for Jerry. He didn't like making cold calls (who does?) and he found every reason to avoid them. When he did make calls he spent most of the time first trying to get the prospect to like him, then trying to prove how smart he was. Both behaviors are primary indicators of need for approval. Jerry was also reluctant to ask for referrals from his many contacts in the industry. He did not want to appear needy.

Jerry wasted lots of time with prospects who never hired him. They sensed he needed to be thought of as smart, so they let him prove it over and over again by picking his brain for valuable information that Jerry should have been charging for. Not wanting to risk annoying his prospect, Jerry never asked any tough or probing questions. He backed off at the first hint of resistance. He didn't talk about money and agreed to write proposals whenever asked. His need for approval caused him a lot of extra work.

Closing was also an issue for Jerry. Needing approval from prospects, he never pushed anything to a conclusion. Every pursuit he ever started was still in his pipeline because there was a slim chance the prospect would come around. Jerry never got the prospect to say, "No." He didn't want to be seen as pushy.

Being well thought of was important to Jerry. He was brought to the brink of asking for help in January when the month ended with no new business closed. He was sure January was going to be a big month because eight prospects told him to call "after the holiday" to get things moving. All eight fell through and Jerry realized there was never anything there.

The final straw occurred in early February when he received a request to provide a proposal for a consulting project. He was to be one of four bidders. Jerry immediately recognized the request for the proposal – he had essentially written it during his initial sales calls! The prospect had taken Jerry's best ideas and along with Jerry himself, asked three others to bid on his ideas. One of the other bidders won the project.

Jerry's frustration was palpable as he sat in our office. We agreed to coach him if he agreed to confront his need for approval. Jerry was motivated. His family depended on him and he wasn't used to failure. He committed himself to confronting his issues.

A slight change in mindset helped him reframe everything. Once he realized that the need for approval was creating many of his problems and exacerbating others, he was ready. We asked Jerry to stop seeking approval from prospects and begin to earn their respect. Jerry also realized that the proper place to get approval was from his spouse and children and his sales coach.

We showed him that the best way to earn respect from prospects was to value what he knew and not give it away for free. He began to understand that prospects expected certain questions from salespeople and that some of the questions would be tough to answer. It was an "ah-ha" moment when a prospect confided that he really respected one of Jerry's competitors and Jerry knew for a fact that the competitor never did free consulting and was tougher on prospects.

Jerry finally got it. Prospects lack respect for salespeople they can push around. By asking probing questions, ending pursuits that were going nowhere, qualifying harder, and closing when the time was right, he won the prospects' respect and began writing business and growing his company. In doing so, he earned an extra "portion" of approval from his family...and his sales coaches.

Over the next year Jerry expended a tremendous amount of emotional energy trying to stop looking for approval from his prospects. We had him take reminder notes on sales calls so that he wouldn't forget to ask the tougher questions. We had him ask prospects to remind him to ask about money before he left. We had him verbalize what he feared when he balked at asking particular questions. Verbalizing helped him realize how unfounded the fears generally were. It was very hard work for Jerry but he was committed. When prospects didn't react negatively as he feared they might, he became more courageous. Little successes built on each other until he realized that he didn't care what prospects thought of him anymore.

Today Jerry's income is triple what his highest salary was when he was employed in a large company. He has a sales process he follows but he never comes across to prospects as a salesperson. He doesn't use techniques per se. He asks questions and prospects answer. No questions are too tough for Jerry to ask. Topics he would not broach with a prospect in the past come up in conversation as a matter of course.

Jerry is one of the most respected professionals in his field. When he is referred or called in, he writes the business 90 percent of the time, without free consulting and wasted proposal efforts. Selling uses up very little of Jerry's emotional energy now and he has more to give those he loves. Jerry is living proof of an amazing paradox.

Once he stopped seeking approval anywhere he started to get approval from everywhere. However, Jerry really doesn't care. His attitude is that approval is nice, but he really doesn't need it.

12

Overcoming Money Weakness

Discomfort in talking about money is one of the most common hidden obstacles and exists in 65 percent of salespeople according to the Objective Management Group, (www.objectivemanagement.com), an industry leader in sales force evaluations and sales candidate screening. Most of us develop inhibitions about discussing money early in life and carry them with us into adulthood and into our selling careers. Thus, most salespeople feel uncomfortable talking about money with a prospect because they view such questions as intrusive and none of their business.

WHAT IS MONEY WEAKNESS?

If you sit down to write a quote or proposal and the prospect has no idea what number will be forthcoming or you don't know what number the prospect is expecting, you might be suffering from <u>money weakness</u>.

Large dollar deals frequently cause salespeople to alter major elements of the selling process. It is important to note that "large" is a relative number and changes over time. When salespeople perceive a deal to be "a big one" they are more prone to cede control of the sales process to the prospect and capitulate to whatever process the prospect wants to use. For example, you might allow them to dictate what questions they will and will not answer or you might chase projects and spend considerable resources without properly qualifying them. When salespeople perceive the project to be "really important" they tend to bring the boss in on the first call; engage technical support too early in the process; prepare white papers and slide presentations before they are warranted; and neglect to discuss the financial aspects of the project early on. These are all symptoms of money weakness.

IDENTIFYING MONEY WEAKNESS

Sticker shock by a prospect is very hard to overcome and frequently causes a prospect who was interested in your product or service to begin to look elsewhere. Sticker shock occurs when a prospect opens a proposal and sees a price much higher than they were expecting. This only happens, however, when money is not discussed before the salesperson agrees to write a quote or proposal.

A salesperson with money weakness will usually not ask about money. In contrast, the Optimal Salesperson never agrees to provide a quote without discussing money ahead of time. This discussion will always have one of two effects. Either it will eliminate the need for a proposal because the prospect does not have enough money or it will set the expectation so that sticker shock does not occur.

Sometimes salespeople don't ask about money because they are uncomfortable with the subject. But sometimes they don't ask because they are afraid to find out that the prospect is unqualified. They would prefer to keep the prospect in their pipeline thinking they will win the business with a killer proposal, overcoming all of the prospect's money objections with a series of cogent, expertly delivered arguments. This causes what author David Kurlan calls <u>pipeline bloat</u>, a pipeline filled with prospects who will never buy, resulting in low closing rates and inaccurate and unreliable forecasts.

Excuses we hear for not talking about money are numerous and sometimes humorous. Follows are some of the most common excuses.

- I forgot to ask. (We understand once, but not 23 times in a row.)

- It wasn't the right time. (It is seldom the wrong time.)

- He didn't know. (Could he find out?)

- They have money; after all this is Exxon, IBM, etc. (Do they have money for this product at this time?)

- The project is funded. (For how much?)

- They don't have a budget. (How will they proceed then?)

- They're working on it. (Who is working on what?)

- Only corporate knows. (So, go ask them.)

- He wouldn't tell me (Why not?)

- I wasn't ready. (I'll take preliminary numbers.)

- I didn't want to upset her. (Why would it?)

- It was too early in the process. (It is never too early.)

- He wasn't the right person. (Who is?)

- We haven't priced it yet. (Who cares? We want to know their numbers.)

- I didn't want to look pushy. (Talking about money is not pushy!)

- I didn't want to give a bad impression. (So you think dancing around the subject will make a good one?)

If you leave sales calls without discussing money and hear yourself use one or more of these excuses, then you probably have a hidden obstacle in dealing with money.

Overpricing projects or continually leaving money on the table is another sign of a possible problem. For example, when your bid is $5,000 and the prospect would have paid $6,000 you left $1000 on the table This usually means that at the proposal preparation time the salesperson is unaware of the price the prospect is expecting. Either the subject was never broached or not specifically mentioned.

The Optimal Salesperson is always prepared to discuss money with a prospect early in the sales cycle. Their sales process demands it and they immediately tackle the task. They focus on making sure the prospect has enough money to move the project forward and that the prospect is willing to pay a premium for perceived value. There is no mystery about money on either side of the transaction and the prospect is not surprised by the price when he or she opens the proposal.

Money tolerance, excitement at the prospect of a "big" opportunity is another facet of money weakness. A salesperson with low money tolerance is competent when the deal involves relatively small dollar amounts. ("Small" being relative, ranging from hundreds to even millions of dollars.) This same person is ineffective with large deals or bigger prospects.

A salesperson suffering from low money tolerance will tend to over-prepare for sales calls on larger projects and call lower in the organization than normal. Because they ask for executive presence or technical help when dollar values loom large in their minds, sales managers can spot this problem easily. The salesperson wants help because they want to be "ready" and to help establish "credibility," code words for, "Help, I'm out of my comfort zone!"

The sales process that a salesperson executes flawlessly on smaller deals will be abandoned on high-dollar deals by a person with low money tolerance. They act overly deferential toward the prospect, agreeing to send information, do demos, and write proposals before the prospect has been properly qualified. They fail to ask tough questions and probe deeply, and may avoid discussing money altogether.

EFFECT OF MONEY WEAKNESS

Writing proposals to prospects who lack sufficient funds to purchase the product or service is a major source of wasted resources and increased overhead. Consider the following case study.

Case Study: XYZ Engineering

XYZ Engineering closed one deal for every 14 proposals. To make matters worse, they were written by project managers who would have been billable had they not been wasting time writing so many useless proposals! After some intensive work in learning how to qualify prospects, their close rate increased to slightly less than 50 percent. Their sales were up 15 percent in a market that was generally down 15 percent or so but the largest savings was in the 11 or 12 proposals they did not write.

The biggest problem they had in qualifying prospects centered on the money issue. Once they were able to discuss money and identify those prospects who were willing to pay, they were able to match the client's price without reducing quality. If they couldn't accomplish the first two, they simply didn't propose.

Pricing of a project without having discussed money beforehand can be anxiety-producing. The results are often overpriced proposals resulting in lost opportunities or money. Consider the following example that contrasts Wimpy Ward, a salesperson with money weakness, with Optimal Olivia, who has a strong money concept.

<u>Example 1 – Wimpy Ward's self-talk as he prepares a price for a consulting service.</u>

Question – "How much will it cost?"

Basic project	$40, 000
We might have to do X, to be safe add	+ $2,000
There might be a delay, to be safe add	+ $6,000
Total	$48,000

<u>Example 2 – Optimal Olivia's self-talk as she prepares a price for the same service.</u>

Question -- "The prospect told me he wants to spend $36,000 for this project, so how can I get it done for $36,000?"

"Basic project would normally cost"	$40, 000
"We can't use Mary on this job. She's too expensive. Joe can handle it. That saves $4000."	- $4,000
"Don't start until all data is in, therefore no possibility of a delay. Put a clause in proposal."	--
Total	$36,000

Notice that the Wimpy Ward and Optimal Olivia were attempting to solve different problems. Also note that the Olivia's process is more rational with less anxiety. Can you imagine the normal salesperson agonizing over whether or not to add any contingencies or trying to decide how to lower the cost?

Overcoming money weakness has other benefits. The internal approval process is probably easier for the Optimal Salesperson. When the boss seeks to add money to the bid, all the Optimal Salesperson has to say is, "No, the prospect won't pay more than $36,000." The normal salesperson will probably allow the bid price to be increased by management, thereby further lessening the probability of success. When the salesperson delivers the $48,000 proposal that is higher that the prospect is expecting, he'll most likely hear the prospect day, "Thanks. It looks good. We'll get back to you in a few days."

Credibility of the salesperson is also undermined when this happens. The excitement and rapport the prospect felt when discussing the project with the salesperson is replaced by disappointment and suspicion after the price is delivered. Conversely, by discussing money with the prospect early in the process, the Optimal Salesperson is able to set the prospect's expectations properly and enhance her credibility when she can meet the agreed-upon price. In Olivia's case, the probability of closing soars while time and energy invested in the proposal process are minimized.

Besides making it harder to get new customers, not being able to discuss money can result in losing existing customers. If an existing customer asks for a quote on a new project and the salesperson fails to discuss up-front costs, the customer may be surprised and disappointed with a price that is too high and then start looking elsewhere for a supplier. A lost customer is a very high price to pay just because you feel uncomfortable talking about money.

Avoiding the discussion of money can also result in more competition. Say you are introduced to a prospect for the first time. The person introducing you gives you a glowing recommendation and gets you in before anyone else. You succeed in getting the prospect excited about your product, your company, and your ability to serve them. In a fit of enthusiasm they ask for a quote and you provide one without discussing money at all. If the prospect is expecting a number like $10,000 and you come in at $10,050, that is probably OK.

But if your number is $14,000, what do you think will happen? If they are like most prospects, they will tell you they have to think it over. While you are waiting for a reply they are checking out other sources. If the competition does its job, you may never hear from the prospect again; except that they gave the business to someone else. If you knew they only wanted to spend $10,000 you might have proposed a different model or solution. Discussing money can keep competition out of the game.

Discomfort in discussing money can result in angry customers if there's a change to an existing project. For example, the customer calls and announces that an additional tank has to be installed by the end of the week to avoid an operational catastrophe. The salesperson gets all the relevant data including an understanding from the client that there will be an extra charge but neglects to discuss the exact cost. The salesperson moves quickly and miraculously convinces the delivery team to compress two weeks' work into four days. They get the tank installed on time to a chorus of rave reviews by the client until the bill for $15,000 arrives. "$15,000!!!" the customer screams, "The other three tanks only cost $8,000 each." The customer is upset and angry because he thinks he has been taken advantage of. This story never ends well. Even if you relent and reduce the price to $8,000 (causing lost revenue), trust has been broken and things will never be the same.

Pricing a project is often a stressful endeavor. Getting together a quote in the absence of any discussion of money with the prospect can cause great anxiety as the preparer vacillates between any or all of the following thoughts.

- We need the work, how low can I bid?

- I don't want to lose money, what contingencies should I account for?

- I don't want the client to think we are ripping them off.

- I don't want to leave money on the table.

- I don't want to look stupid if my bid is too low.

- I don't want to look greedy by bidding too high.

The list could go on and on. But all anxiety disappears if the salesperson tells the estimator that the prospect wants to spend $43,500 and if we can match that we close the deal. Sounds easy, doesn't it? All you have to do is eliminate money weakness on your way to becoming an Optimal Salesperson.

ELIMINATING MONEY WEAKNESS

Part of your job as a salesperson is to discuss money. The Optimal Salesperson realizes that any reluctance in discussing money is rooted in the general belief in the social impropriety of such an action. Therefore, he or she distinguishes between discussing money matters in social situations (often frowned upon) and discussing money in business situations (required). The Optimal Salesperson realizes that if the prospect is going to require him to go through the process of writing a proposal, he has the right to know in advance if the prospect can afford him or is willing to pay for value. Experienced salespeople understand that the pain of proceeding with a prospect without discussing money far outweighs the discomfort of discussing money with the prospect.

Repetition is key to overcoming the money weakness. The more you talk about money, the easier it becomes. At first, prospects may pick up on your discomfort and be somewhat contentious, challenging your right to ask. But if you persist, eventually you will be more at ease and prospects will respond in a more positive manner. Eventually you will be comfortable in asking the prospect about budgets and other money matters. When you ask with the expectation that they will tell you what you want to know…they will. No special techniques required.

Follow the process described in Chapter 10 and use the information in this chapter to adopt the right mindset, and money weakness will quickly disappear. As pervasive as it is in society, it is one of the easier of the major hidden weaknesses to overcome. All you need to do is recognize the problem, be motivated to overcome it, and then face some short-lived and relatively mild discomfort. Then you will become proficient at discussing money. Once you can talk about money comfortably and naturally, you will be miles ahead of most of your competition.

13

Stay in the Moment

Surprises often happen on sales calls. The prospect says or does something that the salesperson is unprepared for. Or the prospect reacts negatively to the salesperson's question or statement. This causes many salespeople to shift their focus from the prospect and what is being said and focus internally as self-talk begins. "I know I shouldn't have said that," they think. For the next several minutes, they mentally check in and out of the sales call, focusing inward for periods ranging from 5-10 seconds to a minute or two.

THE SLIPPERY SLOPE OF FOCUS

The fact that many of these reactions have their roots embedded in our belief systems makes it even more difficult. Unlike some other hidden obstacles, ramifications of not being in the moment are subtle, making it difficult to recognize that the problem even exists. The instinct to focus inwardly is a reflex and most people are unaware they are doing it.

And, even if you do recognize the problem, involuntary reactions are tough to overcome. It is somewhat like trying to teach yourself not to blink when something comes close to your eye.

However, the Optimal Salesperson stays <u>in the moment</u>. They hear what the prospect says and immediately react to it with skills that have been honed thorough constant practice. Consider these examples:

Prospect: "Your price is too high."

Regular salesperson self-talk: "I knew it! We should have quoted model 256-b!"

Optimal Salesperson response: "So what happens next?"

Prospect: "You know I can't tell you the budget."

Regular salesperson self-talk: "I told the boss they wouldn't tell me. Now I look stupid for having asked."

The Optimal Salesperson response: "Why not?"

The exact response is less important than the fact that there is a response. Cues are missed while the salesperson focuses inward and stops paying close attention. When you miss the prospect's cues, you lose the opportunity to control the conversation by asking questions at key points. Not paying attention might cause the average salesperson to fail to hear clues the prospect gives to objections that might come up later in the sales cycle, thus losing the advantage of early detection.

The Optimal Salesperson focuses on the prospect and pays close attention at all times. Thus he or she is able to detect nuances in the prospect's responses that will prompt questions and further discovery, providing the Optimal Salesperson with a decided advantage. In contrast, the average salesperson can miss nuances regarding the problem at hand, and thus his competitive edge.

SYMPTOMS OF NOT BEING IN THE MOMENT

Incomplete understanding of the prospect's situation, also known as missing data are major symptoms of not staying in the moment. When asked, the salesperson is unable to answer simple follow-up questions about what the prospect wants or needs, why they need it or what they are using now. This even happens when salespeople have been coached, resulting in embarrassment and difficulty understanding why they didn't think to ask. This is usually because they were not paying attention to the prospect while they talked to themselves; they missed a cue provided by the tonality, body language, or actual words of the prospect that would have given them an opening to ask a follow-up question.

Sales managers may see this problem clearly if they have two people on the same call. Differences in the reports of the two people might lead you to believe they have been on two separate calls. One of them obviously was not listening.

Other times the data are recorded accurately but context is lacking. It is one thing to hear the prospect say that they need to add a new bedroom to their existing house. A salesperson who was not paying close attention might get the fact that the mother-on-law was moving in but might miss the context that the prospect was a favorite son-in-law who felt a duty to help out. Focus on the mother-in-law aspect and you get one impression. Focus on the favorite son-in-law aspect and you get another. Focus on the feeling of duty and you get a third.

All these have different effects on bedroom design and selection process. And the different nuanced meaning of each may be couched in the tonality or body language of the prospect which might be easily missed if the salesperson is not paying close attention at all times.

Superficial conversations are still another symptom of not being in the moment. The salesperson is inwardly focused and stays at the superficial level because she never sees an opening to ask questions that will get to the prospect's underlying buying motivation. We witnessed a call where the salesperson spent 50 of the 60 minutes talking about flying. (He was a pilot and so was the prospect.) He had tried to ask probing questions early in the call and was rebuffed. Co-author Dan picked out several entry points for further discussion during the debriefing, but our erstwhile salesperson admitted he was mostly thinking instead of paying attention.

Not staying in the moment is usually only detected through skilled questioning. The salesperson is usually unaware of why the sales call went poorly. They blame it on a prospect that didn't really need what they were selling or focus on the competition.

TRAIN YOURSELF TO STAY IN THE MOMENT

Preparation is the best way to prevent losing control of emotions while in front of the prospect. The more prepared you are, the fewer surprises the client can throw at you. Preparation is more than product knowledge and information about the company. It involves anticipating objections as well as hard questions from the prospect. By thinking these through you are better prepared to respond.

Avoid memorization and rote answers, which can sound canned and unnatural. The prospect may have many different ways of coming at you and it's impossible to guess her exact phraseology. Rather, practice the sales techniques you have learned over and over. Have someone role- play with you and ask tough questions in different ways until you can respond automatically without thinking.

In this manner, you can train yourself to respond to the prospect more quickly without shifting your focus inward. Your instinct to revert inward will have passed and the conversation will be moving forward.

This kind of preparation is similar to batting practice. Professional baseball players condition their muscle memory to react to what their eyes see before they have a chance to think about it. They will tell you afterward what they were "thinking" but in reality, they were merely reacting. They recreated the thoughts <u>after</u> the action took place. Role playing in advance of the sales call can accomplish the same result.

STAYING IN THE MOMENT: DISTRACTED DANEEN

Daneen was a management consultant. She worked for years as a department manager in a large organization. Her field was supervisory training for first-line supervisors. She was knowledgeable and had a positive effect on a client's operation when engaged on a project. The problem was that first-line supervisors were not the ones who hired her. To get hired, she had to meet with the CEO of a company that employed between 100-300 people.

Daneen was very uncomfortable in the executive suite. Although she could identify with the problems of the first-line supervisor, she was unable to translate it into how it affected the CEO, making her especially vulnerable to losing control of her emotions on sales calls.

Daneen's income was meager and hardly in line with her excellent performance and results. But her lack of ability to stay in the moment cost her a lot of money. And the problem compounded itself -- the less she made, the lower her confidence got, and the more she was susceptible to self-talk during sales calls.

Although she knew how to sell, she continually failed to execute basic sales techniques and follow her sales process. She was easily distracted by prospects and became even more frustrated during sales training. Initially Daneen blamed her lack of success on not knowing what to say. This was easy for her to accept, since she didn't want to deal with executives anyway.

She usually made a good connection with the prospect but could not answer simple questions during the sales debriefing. She also did fine when the prospect did not challenge her. However, as soon as the prospect said something like, "That seems awfully expensive," or, "Why should I use you and not ABC Company who was in last week?" she clammed up, losing her focus in mental self-talk.

Her sales coach pointed out places where she could have asked a question or made a reply. Daneen was amazed that she didn't recognize those opportunities while on the sales call. It was especially galling since she was a good student and always knew how to handle these situations in class. It became obvious to both her and her coach that she was not staying in the moment while on the sales call. She was not hearing everything the prospect was saying.

Daneen lost credibility with CEOs because she came across as weak. They told her they needed to think about what she had said and that she should get back to them in a couple of weeks. Most salespeople know how that scenario plays out; lots of follow-up calls; maybe a request for a proposal; followed by more put-offs as the prospect thinks about it some more. Then something happens in the economy or the marketplace or a company event and the project is put on the back burner never to be resurrected again.

Daneen and her sales coach practiced intensely for an hour or two before each major sales call. They role-played. First Daneen played the part of the prospect and her coach was the salesperson. This gave her coach a good idea of what her self-limiting beliefs were. Salespeople, when put in the role of the prospect, will act out their worst fears, providing important clues as to what self-limiting beliefs contribute to their problems.

Beliefs turn simple questions by the prospect into tough questions for the salesperson, resulting in failure to stay in the moment. For example, if you are comfortable with the fact that your prices are higher than the competition, and have a supportive buying cycle, that lets you believe that prospects do not buy based on price. Thus, you might expect money questions and handle them easily.   However, if your beliefs around money are weak, then any question about money might send you into a mini-panic attack, causing you to lose focus and engage in self-talk.

Once Daneen's sales coach understood which beliefs were getting in the way, he could begin to condition her mindset. He also helped her craft answers to questions that were likely to trip her up. Then they switched roles and practiced frequently, repeating the same scenario over and over again in several different ways.

Her coach also gave her some sales techniques. For instance, when she "woke up" and realized that she had just missed the last 20 seconds of the conversation, she would ask the customer politely to back up. ("Excuse me sir, I missed that last thing you said. Could you repeat it?") The prospect will usually take responsibility for not expressing the concept clearly and restate the idea, using different words. Daneen also found it useful to "play back" to the prospect what she thought she heard. This helped her confirm the fact that she had not missed anything. ("Am I correct in thinking you are saying …"). She only needed these techniques until she overcame her inability to stay in the moment.

Daneen went into the sales call having handled most of the tough questions she was likely to hear multiple times in different forms. She was ready.

As a result of two months of hard work, a more focused Daneen has had less miscommunication on sales calls and increased close rates. However, other problems keep her from getting to a higher level of performance. She is still uncomfortable calling on CEOs and has difficulty understanding things from their perspective. However, she is earning enough money to remain self-employed, is putting her daughter through college, and has met some financial goals. She reached a plateau and is satisfied for now.

14

How You Buy Affects Your
Selling Effectiveness

Fasten your seat belts and open your mind. You may not agree with what is written in this chapter. Buy cycles are one topic salespeople find more disturbing than any other.

TED'S TOY: SALESPERSON BUY CYCLE

Your buying habits tell a lot about the problems you will encounter in sales. Your <u>buy cycle</u> is simply the process you use when making a major personal purchase. Chapter 3 mentioned salesperson Ted who is looking to purchase a 63-inch, high-definition, flat screen television with a high-end sound system.

His first step is to do some research. He looks up *Consumer Reports* and gets ratings on all major models. Then he starts to shop. He goes to six different stores and compares the features, benefits, and prices for each model. Ted finally decides on a model and a store. But just to make sure, he thinks about it for a couple of weeks and goes back to the store four times before he finally pulls the trigger and orders the unit.

This sequence of research, shopping, and thinking it over is repeated every time Ted makes a major personal purchase. This activity makes Ted's buy cycle <u>non-supportive</u> because it fails to support him when he is in front of a prospect selling his product.

Because of his own personal buy cycle, Ted is vulnerable to prospects who want to put him through a similar process. Because he understands it so well – after all, he uses it himself – Ted finds it difficult to control the sales process when the prospect tries to comparison shop. Since he also buys on price, Ted has hard time focusing on the value his product brings. Additionally, closing is difficult, since he never makes a decision the first time he sees something. However, not all prospects comparison shop, do research, or buy on price. But prospects who do act this way will be a problem for Ted.

<u>Customer empathy</u> is a deadly disease for salespeople, and a non-supportive buy cycle is the source of much customer empathy. Customer empathy leaves you powerless and creates a vicious cycle. The customer says they need to think about it and you let them because, after all, that's what you would do. The fact that one more person shares your method of buying reinforces your belief that thinking it over is the right thing to do. In reality, the only one thinking about this deal until the next time you call is you! How much of the time between your calls to the prospect are they actually mulling over your product or service? Probably only a few minutes in two weeks. This "thinking" could be accomplished while you were still in front of them.

Many people think they can <u>compartmentalize</u>, acting one way when they buy and doing something entirely different when they are selling. Rarely does this work.

Your buy cycle is actually a <u>belief system</u> that operates on an unconscious level. It causes instinctive behavior that is the most difficult to control. Its effects are subtle but powerful. Trying to control the instincts caused by a non-supportive buy cycle is a little like trying to remember to breathe out of your left nostril while you hit a baseball coming at you ninety miles per hour. You might be able to do it, but it hardly makes you a better hitter.

REASONS TO CHANGE YOUR BUY CYCLE

<u>Price objections</u> are especially troublesome for some salespeople. They know they are providing more value to the prospect than the competition. Their colleagues seem to be able to hold their margins. But for some reason, they always seem to find that prospects boil everything down to a decision based on price. Their prospects always seem to want to comparison shop; colleagues never seem to be put through this process by their prospects. Not understanding the problem and not wanting to take responsibility, they figure it probably has something to do with their territory.

It is difficult to convince this salesperson that because they themselves comparison shop they are contributing to the problem. If you take 15 pounds of air out of your left front tire, the car will constantly pull to the left. You, the driver, will be fighting the wheel to keep it straight. Properly inflate the tire and the car will steer a straight course with only a light touch on the wheel.

Although the prospect has no idea that you comparison

shop, you will subtly influence the prospect to take on that behavior. Look around the room you are in right now and try to avoid noticing anything blue. If you are like most people, blue is all you see. The thought was in your head and you couldn't control yourself.

If you are in a highly competitive market where price shopping is endemic, then change how you buy personally and you will be a more effective salesperson. It would be like inflating your left front tire or clearing your mind of thoughts about any particular color.

Put-offs cause a lot of wasted time for salespeople. The "kiss of death" for many deals is that dreaded phrase, "I want to think it over." No matter how big the purchase, the Optimal Salesperson makes quick (as opposed to rash) buying decisions and participates in a <u>supportive buy cycle</u>; that is, a cycle congruent or in tune with his or her own purchasing habits. Let's say Optimal Olivia needs a new sound system for her home. First, she enumerates the performance she desires in terms of sound quality, number of speakers, control mechanisms, and so on. Then she determines how much she is willing to pay for the system. Third, she chooses a retailer who she trusts to make the purchase from. She goes to that retailer and tells them what she is looking for and asks if they have a system that meets her specifications and is within her budget. If they do, she buys it. If they don't, she checks with her second favorite retailer.

When a prospect has arrived at the point in the sales process when they should be making a buying decision because that is what they said they would do; they should say "Yes" or "No." If instead the prospect decides to "think it over," it probably means that they have decided not to buy but are reluctant to either admit it to themselves or feel bad about telling the salesperson.

Many books have been written about closing techniques at this critical point in the sale (Our recommendation: *Baseline Selling* by Dave Kurlan). But you must be willing to use closing techniques in the first place. The Optimal Salesperson with a supportive buy cycle will choose the appropriate technique and get the prospect to say either "Yes" or "No." Non-optimal salespeople with a personal buy cycle that includes thinking over every purchase will capitulate and agree to follow up to get the final decision. They will end up with lots of prospects in their pipeline who are thinking it over but will never buy. They also have a low close rate because time kills deals.

Prospects are frequently overcome by other events while "thinking it over," pushing your purchase to the ever-popular back burner. These deals die a slow and painful death and can suck valuable prospecting time from your schedule.

Because of this, forecasting future sales for non-optimal salespeople is difficult. Their pipelines are bloated with deals that will never close. Assumed probabilities are inflated and are usually based on wishful thinking. Sales targets are missed and more time is wasted with useless explanations to upper management. Worse yet, management decisions can be made based on assumed sales that never come to pass.

The salesperson with a non-supportive buy cycle will also have difficulty in closing deals. The deals that do close will have an elongated sales cycle that causes the expenditure of more time, energy, and money for all concerned. Prospecting time suffers, cash flow is impacted, and profitability is adversely affected.

DEVELOP BUYING HABITS TO SUPPORT
HOW YOU SELL

Many people are incredulous when we ask them to change their purchasing habits to a buy cycle that supports the way they are trying to sell. They feel that it will cost them a lot of extra money. Although shopping around may personally save you a few dollars in the short run, you'll eventually lose more in commissions because you will tolerate the same behavior in your prospects. If you have a non-supportive buy cycle and are experiencing low close rates, comparison shopping by your prospects, and low margins, consider being more congruent with your buying/selling behaviors. Once the new buying process becomes habit, many of your selling problems will disappear.

It takes time however; two and a half years in the case of Marcus in the next section. Most of the effort revolved around convincing Marcus that his buy cycle was causing the problem.

MISERLY MARCUS

Marcus owned a small firm that focused on general contracting for commercial construction. He was motivated and enthusiastic about adopting and adapting a sales process that he could execute expertly. He also worked on overcoming his self-limiting beliefs and was able to grow his business to about $3 million per year.

But then he became stuck. He was continually involved in bidding for work where low price won. He kept his team of estimators busy with a seemingly endless supply of bids to be prepared. Marcus was a tireless prospector and kept the pipeline full. The problem was that margins were thin due to constant bidding and his overhead was high for a small firm. It cost a lot of money to pay staff to prepare all of those bids. And Marcus was getting frustrated and tired from all of the hard work he put in dredging up these seemingly useless opportunities.

However, on a personal level, Marcus was a bargain shopper. It pained him to pay a penny more than the lowest available price. So every time he made a purchase (major or otherwise) he shopped incessantly. Even with his subcontractors, he sometimes got five or six bids and if he thought the price was too high, would often re-bid. When making a purchase for the house, he drove his wife crazy taking forever to make a buying decision and sometimes accepting inferior products or services because it was a "deal."

Meanwhile, closing rates remained abysmal for Marcus. He bid 32 times to one prospect without ever winning work. To a person who believes that low price wins every time, losses were deemed as estimating failures rather than selling failures. Any attempt to suggest otherwise was rebuffed. "Theories are great," he said. "But you have to understand the contracting world. Price wins every time." Even the occasional time he won without being the low bid was viewed as an aberration and not replicable, even when it happened again. Marcus's response to losing was to squeeze the estimates for the next round of bids, further depressing profit margins. His overall sales strategy was to bid, bid, bid, and hope.

So, how to get Marcus to understand that his buy cycle was causing his problems? We asked Marcus to keep a running tabulation of his bids and had him write down the probability of winning each one.

At the end of six months we sat down and reviewed the data. The results were somewhat predictable but startling nonetheless. When he was negotiating, his close rate was 100 percent. When he was bidding, his close rate was 0 percent. This encompassed about 60-70 bids over a six-month period. The close rates were a testament to the quality of his work. We asked Marcus why he continued to bid since it looked as if he already knew which ones he was going win.

Still Marcus refused to believe the empirical data. He wanted even more information before conceding that his buy cycle had an effect upon his selling results. So, after another year of collecting the exact same results, he finally agreed to try and change, thus proving once again that self-limiting beliefs die hard.

Marcus' anxiety rose sharply whenever he talked about how he bought, so we started small. We asked him to go to the store and pick out a tie without looking at the price. When this was suggested to him his reaction was almost funny. He started to pat his chest and got visibly apprehensive. Finally after some coaxing he agreed. He wore the tie proudly to the next training session.

Whenever we discovered that he was in the market for something we intervened to coach him through the buying process so that he did not revert to behaviors that would defeat him when he was in selling mode. A big breakthrough came when it was time for Marcus to buy a car. He and his wife had just had a baby and decided they needed a Volvo. They were ready to pick out the car in the showroom and Marcus had backed out at the last minute because he thought the price was a couple of hundred dollars too high. His wife became very angry with him.

It wasn't really the money; just his non-supportive buying habits kicking in again. He became even more upset with himself when it was pointed out that for a very small sum his wife was upset, his new baby was riding in more jeopardy than he or his wife were comfortable with, and he was going to have to waste even more time to try to save $200. When he lamented, "Why do I do this to myself?" we knew that the moment of change had finally occurred.

Marcus called up the dealer and purchased the car for the last price discussed. Once he saw the light, he solidified his new buying habit in a couple of months. And dramatic changes took place in his business as well.

Close rates sky rocketed to near 100 percent. Rather than getting better at bidding he simply stopped bidding. If he ascertained early in the process that the prospect was going to go through a bidding process, he declined to participate. All of his business now came through as noncompetitive negotiated contracts.

He only worked with people who valued the quality he brought to the projects and were willing to pay for it. Since he stopped the bids, he eliminated his estimating staff entirely. He prepared the proposals for clients who wanted to negotiate with him. Estimating was easy since there was no pressure to come in with the lowest number, as he always knew the number the client was looking for before he sat down to do his proposal.

He also eliminated the bidding processes with subcontractors since he knew who the best ones were and worked with them exclusively. They gave Marcus fair and reasonable prices when he asked for them.

Marcus' business grew by over 33 percent with revenue in excess of $4 million each year. So the end result of changing his buy cycle was a 33 percent increase in sales, dramatically increased margins, and reduced staff. Marcus now only works four days a week and when he fishes, it's for actual trout or bass, rather than prospects that got away.

A Lesson Learned

Marcus' buy cycle issues were especially severe but sadly, somewhat common. Non-supportive buy cycles cause people to harbor deep, self-limiting beliefs with far-reaching effects. The cost is huge, and can be measured not only in dollars but relationships, quality of work and home life, stress, and more.

The benefits of a supportive buy cycle are profound. So if you are experiencing problems related to buy cycle at least think about trying to change the way you buy. You have only a few dollars to lose and everything to gain.

15

Self-Limiting Beliefs vs. Reality

<u>Beliefs</u> are firmly held convictions about the way things are. A belief becomes <u>self-limiting</u> when it gets in the way of success. Believing that red wine should be consumed with pasta probably won't hinder you from sales success but believing that people always buy based on price will have an effect on your bottom line.

WHICH IS WHICH?

Self-limiting beliefs are sometimes difficult to detect because, as far as the person with the belief is concerned, there is no doubt about its veracity. The belief coincides with her experience and she can point to many examples to prove that her view is the correct one.

Self-limiting beliefs present obstacles to sales success that are hidden; a person's beliefs are not always obvious on the surface. It's amazing how many salespeople can hold onto a self-limiting belief in the face of reality. They ignore facts that conflict with their belief and ascribe outside causes to explain the success of salespeople who hold contrary beliefs. You hear them explain away someone else's success by saying, "Of course they were willing to pay more in California, Its different there." But if they moved to California they would explain failure away by saying, "Well, Los Angeles is different than San Francisco. They have more money up there."

Understanding reality is the first step to overcoming a self-limiting belief. However, to overcome the belief, you need more than to just hear the reality. Proving reality to a person holding a belief to the contrary is extremely difficult. The person owning the belief usually discounts most of the best arguments by saying that the facts don't apply in this case, by questioning the facts, by declaring your facts to be the exception to the rule, or by declaring their case to be the exception to the rule. When all else fails, they use the ever popular, "you just don't understand my business" all-purpose excuse for ignoring reality.

Chapter 10 discussed the general process for overcoming hidden obstacles, and Step 4 in that chapter described specific suggestions for adopting the proper mindset. Be careful as you read the following sections, however. If you have the self-limiting belief being described, you may disagree with what is written. If you find yourself thinking one of the excuses given below, you may actually have the belief. At least consider it as a possibility rather than immediately writing it off as "someone else's problem."

I MUST CALL ON PURCHASING AGENTS FIRST

The Self-Limiting Belief

"Buyers buy stuff, I sell stuff. I have to call on them. It's a rule." Many salespeople hold this basic belief. It's also the primary reason why these same salespeople end up in bidding situations where low price wins every time. They find it hard to differentiate their product from anyone else's. They won't call elsewhere in the organization because they don't want to "get off on the wrong foot" or just think that ultimately they will end up back in purchasing so, "What's the use of calling anywhere else?"

The Reality

As a rule, purchasing agents don't care who they buy from. Their job is to get the best price as long as you meet or exceed the specification. The right place to call is the person in the organization who owns the problem your product or service is designed to fix. If you sell computer technology, that would be the head of the information technology department who may be struggling with down time due to old equipment. Or the VP of operations who can't get product out the door because his control system is antiquated. Both of these individuals might ultimately have to go through the purchasing department, and purchasing may impose a competitive "bid" process. But having gotten in at the source of the problem before the requisition gets to purchasing, the Optimal Salesperson can help the prospect define criteria to be used for selection. He or she might even be able to drive the procurement to a sole source -- guess who?

The normal salesperson hears one of two possible answers from purchasing. "We don't have any current requisitions for that" or, "Your timing is good. We can add you to the bid list." Meanwhile the Optimal Salesperson has either written the order or established herself as the one to beat.

ASKING ABOUT MONEY IS NONE OF MY BUSINESS

The Self-Limiting Belief

Money is a charged topic in our society that is generally not discussed in detail. When a friend tells you that he got a great deal on a new car, he has to be really close for you to ask how much he paid. Asking about money is thought to be intrusive and in some cases boorish, crass, and uncouth. A conversation about personal finances is generally thought to be inappropriate in most circles; no one discusses how much they make with anyone else.

The Reality

Discussing personal finances with your neighbor may violate accepted social behavior but failure to discuss money at the appropriate time with a prospect is dereliction of a salesperson's duty. You wouldn't interrogate your neighbor about his health problems either, but if you were a physician and he was your patient, you'd be guilty of malpractice if you failed to ask such personal questions. The Optimal Salesperson knows the difference between social situations in which certain questions are prohibited and business situations in which the same questions are required. If a prospect asks you to expend corporate resources to estimate price or make a presentation, you have an obligation to ask about money to be sure they have enough to afford your product or service. The rules applying to social situations regarding money are irrelevant in selling situations.

I BUILD CREDIBILITY BY IMPRESSING THE PROSPECT WITH HOW MUCH I KNOW

The Self-Limiting Belief

Knowledge of one's product line is essential to sales success. Salespeople without product knowledge are seldom credible. However, most salespeople spend a good portion of their time trying to build credibility by demonstrating their knowledge. They try to prove how much they know by imparting as much information as possible to the prospect. Implicit in this approach is the belief that building credibility is a matter of keeping focus on me, my concerns, and my product. The more I know, the smarter I am, the more the prospect will trust what I say. Hence my credibility is established by telling what I know.

The Reality

Salespeople who act this way have it exactly backwards. You can tell more about what you know by the questions you ask than by the statements you make. Asking questions is the best way to establish credibility. Say you are considering two different contractors to design and build a deck in your backyard. The situation can be handled in two ways:

Scenario 1

You: "I am interested in a deck."

Contractor 1: "You have come to the right place. We have 23 years experience with decks. We have a five-person design team. We are experienced with wood and plastic. We built a deck for three of your neighbors as well as Senator Smith. You really should never use a plastic material because it fades."

Scenario 2

You: "I am interested in a deck."

Contractor 2: "For what reason?"

You: "We like to have parties and are hosting a wedding."

Contractor 2: "How big of deck are you thinking?"

You: "Not sure. Maybe to accommodate 25 people?"

Contractor 2 (noticing the terrain): "Do you get any flooding in your backyard?"

You: "How did you know? We always get flooding after a heavy rain."

Contractor 2: "Did you have a preference for a particular material?"

You: "Our neighbor got a plastic type that we liked."

Contractor 2: "Are you concerned about the color fading?"

You: "We want it to look new. Why?"

Of course, each of the questions Contractor 2 asks would probably have two or three follow-up questions. However, most people would say that Contractor 2 comes across as more credible due to his depth of understanding and specific questions. His product knowledge allows him to anticipate problems and ask questions to get the prospect to share any potential issues or particular requirements.

Also, Contractor 2 engaged you in a conversation about your project. At some point, Contractor 2 will explain how he will approach the project, but only after he has a complete understanding of the prospect's concerns. Subject matter knowledge is most useful if it provides a basis from which to anticipate the prospect's problems and formulate questions that will cause the prospect to share their concerns.

REJECTION IS A BAD THING

The Self-Limiting Belief

Fear of rejection causes salespeople to put off prospecting for new business. It elongates the sales cycles because salespeople avoid asking hard questions and even closing lest they get a "No." When a prospect says they do not want to buy, many salespeople take it personally. For these and other reasons, rejection is viewed as a bad thing.

The Reality

Products and services are rejected, not people. The Optimal Salesperson understands this and does not take rejections personally. Although rejection is never easy, you can deal with it if you <u>reframe</u> it; that is, view it in a different context or perspective. Consider the fact that Thomas Edison tried and failed over a thousand times to design the filament that would make a light bulb work. When asked how he withstood so much failure he replied, "What failure? I just discovered one more material that would not work," He had the proper framework for what he was doing.

Consider the following reasons why rejection can be good and even useful:

- When they say "No," I can move on without wasting any more time. If my product is going to be rejected, the sooner the better.

- When people say "No" I can try out some of new sales techniques. Maybe the next time I'll get a "Yes."

- A "No" now is better than a "No" later preceded by five, "I need to think it over's" and the attendant wasted time.

- "No" toughens me up for bigger prospects to come.

- If my closing rate is one out of three, I need the two "Nos" as much as I need the one "Yes.'

- In the short term, my closing rate is constant. Therefore, to double my sales I need to double the amount of rejections I get. More rejections can equal more money for me.

With the right mindset, "No" is not seen as rejection but rather as part of the selling process and just another step on the way to sales success.

I HAVE A LONG SALES CYCLE

The Self-Limiting Belief

"This industry has a long sales cycle. There is nothing I can do about it." Unsuccessful salespeople buy into this belief and use it as an excuse for just about everything. Granted, selling multimillion dollar service contracts to the Federal Government takes longer that selling new carpeting to a home owner. But most salespeople believe that they have no control over the length of the process. They also believe sales cycle is fixed and invariable and therefore make little effort to shorten it.

The Reality

Hurricane Katrina devastated the Gulf Coast in 2005. Within weeks the Federal Government let billions of dollars of contracts for temporary housing and engineering services among many other things. Normal procurement cycles were cut from many months to days and weeks. Why? Because the urgency of the situation demanded it. Admittedly this was a unique situation but the principle is the same. If you find or create enough urgency, you can cause the client to accelerate their buying process. Get in early enough and create this urgency and you can not only help dictate a shorter cycle but set yourself up as the team to beat. If you wait until a request for proposal comes out to approach the client, the procurement cycle will already be set.

Many times, especially when the client lacks a fixed and predetermined process, the length of the sales cycle is highly variable. The Optimal Salesperson can use several techniques to speed up the process. One is to never leave a meeting without setting up the next. This alone can shorten the process by weeks. Another is to concentrate on developing urgency in the mind of the prospect. However, none of these will be useful (or even tried) unless the salesperson sees the sales cycle as flexible and hence able to be shortened.

I MUST EDUCATE THE PROSPECT

The Self-Limiting Belief

"Educated prospects who know all about my product will do the logical thing and buy it." "If they only knew how well my product was made, they would buy it." "Prospects expect to be educated. It's my job to teach them what they need to know." All of these mindsets limit the success of the salesperson. Owning this belief will cause the salesperson to do a lot of unpaid consulting. In addition, the salesperson who focuses on educating the prospect will most likely not be asking the proper questions to qualify the prospect.

A person with this belief will most likely come back from sales calls saying things like, "They loved us." "They were excited." "They asked a lot of questions," and so on. However, they will be unable to answer any detailed questions about the prospect because the salesperson was talking the whole time.

The Reality

The prospect only needs <u>relevant information</u> about the product; that is, information that solves a problem the prospect is having or answers questions the prospect is wondering about. As described in Chapter 8, the Optimal Salesperson uses a selling process that focuses on the prospect, not the product or service being offered.

Earlier in this chapter we stated that the real purpose of knowing your subject area thoroughly is to allow you to anticipate problems the prospect might have and to craft questions to get the prospect to share those problems with you.

The reality is that the prospect doesn't really care about you, your company, or your product or service. They care about themselves and their problems. Their only involvement is to the extent that you can help them and this where educating the prospect can actually hurt. For instance, when I buy carpet I may only care about how long it will last (plus color, texture, and stain resistance). If a salesman bent my ear about the chemical process that make the carpet last longer, I may start to worry about whether the carpet will cause cancer. That could delay or kill the sale (or me!).

The Optimal Salesperson holds the empowering belief that prospects should be told what they need to know to make a decision -- no more, no less. Don't withhold information, but avoid making it a mission to educate all prospects about all aspects of a product or service.

I DON'T NEED A STRONG RELATIONSHIP TO SELL THE PROSPECT

The Self-Limiting Belief

Many salespeople ignore the process of building a relationship with a prospect believing that "the product sells itself"; Or that, in the end "only price matters most."

The Reality

Connecting to the prospect is imperative and the Optimal Salesperson excels at developing bonding and rapport quickly. But the Optimal Salesperson also knows that the purpose of developing this relationship is to establish a conduit over which information can flow from the prospect to the salesperson. The stronger the relationship, the more information will be exchanged. Very strong relationships will yield high fidelity information that may not be shared with the competition. Or, to put it in terms of the Internet, develop a stronger connection with the prospect than the competition and then the content you can "download" will be richer, more detailed and faster.

HIDDEN OBSTACLES TO SPECIFIC PARTS OF THE SELLING PROCESS

16

Hidden Obstacles to Cold Calling

The thought of making cold calls is one of the scariest things about sales. The prospect of having to approach people they don't know keeps many out of the profession.

COLD CALLING: HOW? WHEN?

Walking into a place of business unannounced and attempting to speak to a decision-maker is one form of cold calling. You must be seeking out someone of authority, because the salesperson who drops off literature is merely providing a delivery service better accomplished by the post office. Another form of cold calling is phoning someone in an attempt to speak to a person with the authority to buy.

In some industries, like commercial real estate, walking in is the preferred method. In other industries such as selling contract engineering services, the telephone is most often used. If distance is an issue, then obviously the telephone is more efficient. In most industries where the salesperson is in the local vicinity of the prospects, either way will work. So salespeople should use whichever way is most comfortable and effective for them.

Consistent daily prospecting should be the norm for the successful salesperson, especially when building a new territory or introducing a new product. Pipelines should build steadily and prospecting should be done on a regular, organized basis. Although prospecting does not always mean cold calling, it usually does in the beginning. Salespeople in the in-between stage also need to cold call to fill in the gaps and keep the pipeline full enough to meet sales goals. However, most top salespeople have developed a network of contacts that provide enough high-quality introductions to keep the pipeline filled. Because of this, they do the least amount of cold calling.

If you find yourself procrastinating when it comes to cold calling or if your pipeline is constantly weak, requiring heroic efforts or unreasonable close rates at the end of each quarter to make your numbers, then you might have one or more of the following hidden obstacles to cold calling.

THE FEAR OF REJECTION

<u>Rejection</u> is the mother of all fears. It is the most obvious of the hidden obstacles and the primary reason why many people avoid a career in sales. Salespeople who suffer from fear of rejection avoid situations where they might hear a prospect say "No." Cold calling has more "No's" associated with it than any other part of the sales cycle. A lack of cold calls is a sure-fire sign of this hidden weakness that both you and your sales manager can spot immediately.

The following are symptoms of fear of rejection:

- When you are required to cold call and find yourself procrastinating.

- Being timid when you get a prospect on the phone

- Accepting put-offs while cold calling.

- Getting a knot in your stomach when thinking about making a cold call.

Fear of rejection is a double-edged sword. It is one of the most difficult aspects of selling to get used to but also one of the primary reasons salespeople get paid so handsomely. They can do what others are afraid of -- put themselves in a position to be rejected day after day.

Overcoming the Fear

Think about what happens when you are rejected. Are you physically hurt? No. You might say your feelings are hurt when they reject you, but what does that mean? That they dislike you personally or think you're a bad person by selling the product? And therein lies the answer. They are not rejecting you, they are rejecting the product or service you're trying to sell.

So what is there to be afraid of? With rejection, not much. If having someone occasionally hang up on you or to tell you to go away is the worst thing that has ever happened, then you've been pretty lucky.

The best way to overcome this or any other fear is to feel the fear and do it anyway. Let the worst thing you can imagine happen to you and you will soon realize two things. First, the worst rarely happens and second, when it does, the consequences are not nearly as catastrophic as your imagination would have you believe.

The one thing you do <u>not</u> want to do is wallow in the fear. That will give your imagination time to magnify it and make it far worse than it really is. When you feel the fear of rejection coming on, recognize that the genetic purpose of fear is to put our bodies on alert to perform at their best. Fear in the case of cold calling is your body's way of telling you to move forward because you are ready for action.

PROSPECTS ARE MEAN AND NASTY AND EAT SALESPEOPLE FOR BREAKFAST

The Self-Limiting Belief

Imagining your prospect as an ogre looking for a chance to reject anyone who dares call would deter anyone from picking up the phone. Many new salespeople view cold calling this way. The target prospect is regarded as someone to be feared. The salesperson sees themselves as an intruder and the prospect as a very important person who despises salespeople and treats them all badly. This attitude will magnify any fear of rejection the salesperson might have. Hence, the symptoms are similar to those given for fear of rejection.

The Empowering Mindset

The truth is that they are not waiting for you at all. Most of the time they are dealing with problems in running their business. For all you know, they are sitting around discussing a problem that your product or service could fix. Plus if you met them on the street or at a party you would think of them as regular people. (And the party or social gathering might be a good way to network or get referrals.) People are people, and if you approach them with respect and dignity you will be treated similarly.

Case Study: Joyce

A new salesperson, Joyce was reluctant to make cold calls. One day she stumbled into the branch office of a company owned by Harvey. Joyce had never met Harvey, but she knew he was the CEO of a medium-sized company and one of Joyce's target prospects. She asked for him by name and was told by the office manager that he was in the home office about ten miles away.

Joyce was happy that the ordeal of the cold call was over and said she would stop by later. The office manager said, "Why don't you use our phone and call him from here?" Although Joyce tried to wriggle out of it, the overly helpful office manager insisted. Much to her surprise she got Harvey on the phone; he suggested that she stop by his office on her way home which of course she was pleased to do.

After a 45-minute meeting, it was obvious to both Joyce and Harvey that Joyce's service did not fit his company's needs. However, he was impressed with her and suggested two other companies where he thought she could help. He offered to introduce her to his contacts there.

This encounter totally changed Joyce's concept of who was behind the doors she was knocking on. She began to imagine the prospects as people who might need what she had and would be glad she called on them. Her call reluctance was greatly reduced and she went on to great success in her sales career.

S/HE WON'T PICK UP THE PHONE

The Self-Limiting Belief

Imagining your prospect to be too busy is closely related to viewing him/her as an ogre. The symptoms are similar but for different reasons. In this case, the salesperson overthinks the problem. Every time they think about making a sales call, they imagine the prospect in the middle of an urgent task and figure that later would be a better time. Later never comes. This is a form of customer empathy. You hate to be bothered when you are in the middle of something and are sure the unknown, unnamed prospect feels the same way, only more so, since he has a much more important job. Since the prospect won't pick up the phone, why bother to call?

The Empowering Mindset

Everyone has a minute to spare, even on days when they are under the gun and every second seems precious. But everyone, including high-ranking executives, has days with plenty of spare minutes. As business owners and homeowners, the authors have taken many sales calls we were glad to receive and helped us out. Granted, there were many others that did not interest us. But a minute here or there to listen did not disrupt our lives in any significant way. If you have a professional approach and act in a calm and upbeat manner, you will be well-received by most. If not, it's their loss. Move on to the next prospect.

Case Study: Ken

In his first month as an engineering salesperson, Ken was given the name of Rick, a VP of a manufacturing company. A combination of fear of rejection and the belief that the VP was too important and busy to talk prevented Ken from calling him. After 3 months of procrastination, Ken lost Rick's contact information.

Years later, Rick was president of a different business and met Ken at one of our sales training sessions. Ken and Rick hit it off. When the topic of prospecting and call reluctance came up, Ken shared the story of how he had been given Rick's name a number of years ago but never called because he thought Rick would be too busy to talk to him. Rick replied that he wished Ken had called because he had some problems Ken could have helped with. This did more to cure Ken's call reluctance than anything we could have told him!

IT'S THE WRONG TIME TO CALL

The Self-Limiting Belief

It is always the wrong time to call in the mind of some salespeople. The following thoughts are used as excuses for not picking up the phone:

- "It's Monday morning, they are too busy. I had better wait until later."

- "Never call before 9 AM - they have to get their day started."

- "Never call between 11 and 2. They are probably at lunch."

- "Friday afternoons are bad times in general because they are trying to end up the week."

- "Do not call between Thanksgiving and Christmas. It is the busiest time of the year."

- "Summer is bad. People are off and/or they are busy."

To listen to these salespeople you would think that the only time to make a sales call is March 3 between three and four in the afternoon. This belief is sometimes just the rationale salespeople use when they actually have a fear of rejection. The result is the same…no calls.

The Empowering Mindset

Lunch is a great time to call. The boss works through lunch but the gatekeepers are gone. Many times an inexperienced gatekeeper is covering the desk during lunch. They are easier to get through. Early morning is great. Maybe the gatekeeper starts later in the day. Maybe the boss comes in early to get a head start. Late in the day is a great time to call, especially after gatekeepers have left.

The holidays are a terrific time to make sales calls. Everyone is in a good mood because it's a happy time of year. There are lots of parties to go to so people don't travel as much. They are more likely to be in their office than on the road. If you think hard enough you can come up with a reason why every hour of every day is the absolute <u>best</u> time to call.

If you hear yourself using any of the previously-mentioned excuses not to call, just adopt the opposite mindset. If you believe it is a good time to call, you will be more effective. The fact is, every one organizes their time differently, so who knows exactly when the best time to call is? Cold calls are random shots in the dark. So you might as well pick the more empowering of the two mindsets. In reality, no time is any better than any other so you might as well go ahead and make the calls.

THEY PROBABLY DON'T NEED IT

The Self-Limiting Belief

Weak salespeople think about how relatively few people actually need what they sell. They may never express this attitude out loud but it is in the back of their mind. It doesn't matter whether they sell one product that few people use or many products that everyone uses, this thought permeates their minds and actions and can even affect some stronger salespeople when things are not going well.

When this attitude is occupying your mind, it reduces your sense of urgency. Other tasks become higher priority. This is a tough belief for a sales manager to spot since few will likely admit it, especially to their boss. But the salesperson should be able to pick it up easily by "listening" to self-talk. You can actually be telling yourself, "This person (or company) probably does not need this. They probably already have one." every time you make a call.

The Empowering Mindset

Forget need. Focus on problems. People do not necessarily know what they need but they do know what problems they have. Cold calling is the process of sifting through the entire list of prospects in your territory and determining who has a problem that your product or service can fix. For example, you might not know you need a lawn service. But you do know you hate dandelions and never seem to be able to get the weed killer down in time. Plus your brother the landscaper always promises to come but never seems to show up.

To defeat this obstacle, spend some time identifying reasons why people need what you sell. Ask your clients why they bought. Ask other salespeople what drives their clients' purchases. You could even do a survey in your territory to find out who has problems your product or service is designed to fix.. You might discover there are many more prospects than even you can handle.

GATEKEEPERS ARE A PROBLEM

The Self-Limiting Belief

Unsuccessful salespeople see gatekeepers as the enemy with whom they are constantly in a pitched battle for survival. Gatekeepers are ruthless, tough, unforgiving, protective, unreasonable, and sometimes downright nasty. Therefore you need to be on the defense when talking and dealing with them.

The Empowering Mindset

Nice people take jobs as gatekeepers. If you met them at a party, you would find them to be grandmothers, wives with children who go to your kids' school, recent college graduates, and so on. In short, gatekeepers are regular people with a job to do. They are not there to keep you out but rather to direct you to the right person. In your case, that happens to be their boss.

Gatekeepers are never told, "If anyone calls with a solution to any of my problems, do not let them get through to me, under any circumstances. I want to solve this problem by myself." If the gatekeeper knew how much time and aggravation you could save the boss, they would let you speak to her right away.

So instead of regarding the gatekeeper as the enemy, look upon them as a potential ally. They have the keys to the kingdom and you both have the same goal: To help their boss run the business more efficiently. Enlist their support: What would be the most convenient time for you to call? Would email be a better way for the initial contact (also offer to copy the gatekeeper on the email – they will be more willing to cooperate.) Share your goals with them and enlist their support. You expect to get through to the person you need to speak to, and they can help.

You probably have a friend somewhere who has a gatekeeper. When you call your friend do you expect to get through if she is in the office? Absolutely. As an experiment, call your friend with the gatekeeper and record the call. Now make a cold call to a prospect that employs a gatekeeper and record that as well. Compare the recordings. What is the difference in attitude? If you are like most people, the call to your friend has a much more relaxed and friendly approach. Adopt that attitude, and you likely will get through much more often.

LISTEN TO YOURSELF

Chapter 14 discussed how the manner in which you buy things can affect the way you sell. The same principles apply to cold calling. When salespeople call you, what do you do? If you are like most, you immediately become irritated and try to get rid of the call. What you should do is listen intently and decide if it is anything you are interested in. If so continue. If not, say "No" and move on. This will help condition your mindset for when you make cold calls and will find its way into your attitude and tone of voice. Both prospects and gatekeepers will pick up on the positive "vibes" and treat you accordingly.

17

Hidden Obstacles to Getting Referrals and Introductions

Growing a business rapidly and profitably depends on the ability to generate a consistent flow of high-quality referrals and introductions. Salespeople can get in their own way when it comes to prospecting by referral.

IDENTIFYING THE PROBLEM

Everyone gets a referral or an introduction occasionally. They can happen without any action on the part of the salesperson. When referrals happen spontaneously, no hidden obstacle comes into play. However, to be truly successful, a salesperson must systematically and continuously seek referrals and introductions. Hidden obstacles within the salesperson frequently inhibit the process of employing a system that will generate referral flow.

Control and preparation are two factors that distinguish between a referral and an introduction. Both referrals and introductions require a "referrer" to act on your behalf to connect you with a potential new customer. However, it is an introduction when a friend referring you prepares the prospect for you and gives you control of the next interaction. As an example, your friend calls you and says, "I talked to Mary, the owner of the hair salon in town. She is unhappy with her accountant who did a sloppy job on her taxes. I told her you were excellent. She wants to meet you and is expecting your call." Introductions like this are easy to close.

However, in another case, your friend might call and say, "I think you should call Mary. I was at a meeting the other day and she was complaining about her accountant. Here is her number." Or your friend might tell Mary to call you and give her your number saying, "Nancy is a great accountant. She does all of my work and is very precise." The last two scenarios are <u>referrals</u> You will still only close about 20 percent because in the first case your friend did not prepare the prospect for your call so it is one step away from a cold call. In the second case, you didn't even know about it and are thus dependant on Mary picking up the phone and calling you which may or may not happen.

Cold calls are a barometer of whether you have hidden weaknesses affecting your ability to get referrals. If you get most of your new prospects by cold calling, then you are either new in sales or have a problem. Weak pipeline is another indicator of a problem; it takes much more time and effort to generate sales by cold call than by referral and introduction.

<u>Procrastination</u> is still another sign. Symptoms include the sense that it is never the right time to ask, avoidance of asking because the possible rejection seems worse than making a cold call, and asking in a timid manner, with the hope that they will be one of the few who would be willing to help.

If you ask confidently and with the expectation that your request will be received well and honored if at all possible, then that is what will likely come to pass. However, if it is taking too much time to fill your pipeline because of a lack of referrals, then you might have one of the hidden weaknesses discussed in the sections below.

HIDDEN OBSTACLES TO ASKING FOR REFERRALS

The Self-Limiting Belief

Fear is one of the biggest reasons salespeople don't ask for referrals. They see asking for referrals as intrusive and imposing on the prospect's good nature. They are afraid of being seen as "pushy." This problem is similar to a fear of rejection but is also related to a large need for approval. In some cases, the fear of asking for a referral is worse than the fear of making a cold call. The salesperson is more worried about ruining an existing relationship by asking for a referral than being rejected outright by a stranger. Although it may be tempting to figure out why this is so, it's more important to recognize the problem and concentrate on fixing it.

The Reality

Friends are always willing to help friends. If not, then what kind of friend are they? Clients who are happy with your work are only too happy to tell others about you. It's in their best interest to do so. If you sold them a product or performed a service for them that works really well, then they will tell other people because they can brag about what a good decision they made in deciding to go with you. It is very common to hear, "We used Charlie to design our website. He is the best graphic designer in the city." You never hear someone say "Don't you just love our new kitchen? Norma designed and installed it. She is one of the worst in the city but we got lucky."

Referrals are like icebergs. Depending on the specific gravity of the water, about 90 percent of an iceberg floats below the surface. Referrals work similarly. For every referral that actually reaches you, there are many more referrals that people are trying to give you that never reach you. If you have ever asked for a referral and had a client say, "I gave your name to Edna, has she called you yet?" you know this phenomenon exists. If you ask for referrals or work with clients on how to effectively refer you (see Chapter 7), you can tap into your already existing base of referrals.

<u>Entitlement</u> is another mindset to adopt in getting referrals. This is not entitlement in the sense that a person feels they should get something based on the sheer essence of their being without doing anything. Rather it's the entitlement that comes from working hard for a client and going above and beyond to help them gain a successful outcome. Most would agree that the salesperson is entitled to get rewarded for the extra effort. Clients and friends sincerely want to help you and you deserve to be helped. Adopt this mentality and you will be able to build your business on referrals alone.

HIDDEN OBSTACLES TO GETTING INTRODUCTIONS

The Self-Limiting Beliefs

<u>Low self-concept</u> is a major obstacle to getting introductions. Asking a client or a friend to proactively seek out people they can introduce seems to the person with low self-concept to be a lot of trouble. "Who would do that for me," they think. "It's too much to ask." In addition most salespeople

don't know how to ask for an introduction (see Chapter 7 for additional information).

The Reality

Who wouldn't give you an introduction? After all, your company does good work. You have products that work well and perform better than advertised. You are an attentive salesperson and on several occasions have gone over and above the call of duty to help the customer out of one jam or another. Why wouldn't they want to introduce you to their associates? They will often brag about who they use to get certain jobs done or what a terrific decision they made in buying your product.

Many people enjoy helping others who have run into similar problems because it gives them a good feeling to demonstrate their knowledge of the industry. They can tell how they solved the problem; they become a bit of a hero for helping someone else out. This is the reality in most cases and an absolute reality for your best customers. It is the mindset of the Optimal Salesperson.

HIDDEN OBSTACLES TO GETTING REFERRALS ON COLD CALLS

The Self-Limiting Beliefs

If a person gives you a <u>lead</u>, they are pointing you at a person who has, might have, or at least occupies a position that usually experiences the type of problems that you solve. Making cold calls is basically a shot in the dark. You have a list of prospects but you don't actually know who has a problem, or who will be receptive to your solution. That is why the hit rate on cold calls is so low. But a lead changes things. If you already know someone has a problem, the probability of success is much higher independent of your skill in actually executing the cold call. It's the difference between fishing in any body of water and fishing in a lake filled with the type of fish you are trying to catch.

After making an unsuccessful cold call, you have invested some time and some energy. You could call the next person on the list and start over or you could try to leverage the time and energy you have already invested into improving the hit rate on your next call. The Optimal Salesperson will always opt to increase the odds for success. All of this seems pretty logical. So why don't more people ask for referrals on unsuccessful cold calls?

<u>Acceptance of average performance</u> is the primary hidden weakness that keeps salespeople from asking for referrals on cold calls. If the prevailing mindset is that a low hit rate is to be expected, and "you just have to make a lot of calls because it is a numbers game" then that is exactly what you will get. Most salespeople's view of what should happen on sales calls is colored by how they react when someone calls them.

One of the first questions we ask new clients is how they react when they receive a cold call. In nearly every case, the person hangs up or immediately tries to get rid of the caller. With that as a frame of reference, it is no wonder that most salespeople make a cold call with the attitude that the prospect will try to get rid of them immediately and will not be in any frame of mind to give a referral. Even if they give one it will be a lousy lead anyway, so they believe, so what the use of asking. In addition to these mindsets, fear of rejection and need for approval also get in the way of asking for referrals on cold calls.

The Reality

"Why not ask" is what the Optimal Salesperson says. "What have I got to lose? The worst they can say is 'No.'" If you think about it, one way for the prospect to get you off his or her neck is to sic you onto someone else. A bad lead is better than a good cold call. "I spent all this time (three minutes) trying to bond and explaining what I do, I might just as well get something for my trouble." These statements describe the mindset of a cold caller who will shortly have no more time for cold calls, as she will soon be flooded with leads, referrals, and introductions.

Case Study: Richard

Richard was a rookie Realtor trying to break into the business. He was an experienced tree trimmer and knew nothing about selling. After taking our class on cold calling, he cold called a woman and asked if she was interested in listing her house for sale. Not surprisingly the woman said, "No." Richard then asked if she knew anyone who was and the woman said her daughter might be, and gave Richard her number when he asked for it.

This was a <u>lead</u> because he had no relationship with the mother, and the mother did not introduce him or give permission to use her name as a referral. It turned out, however, that the daughter was interested in buying a house with her fiancé. He ended up selling her a house and listing both the fiancé's house and the daughter's house for sale. Asking for the referral resulted in three transactions with a total commission worth tens of thousands of dollars.

But wait, as the TV infomercial says, there's more. Guess what occupation the mother was in? She was the receptionist in a residential real estate office. There were probably ten agents in the back room trying to figure out where there next transaction was coming from and their receptionist gave three away to a person who cold called.

Asking is the key factor. It adds no extra time. It is easy to do. There is no special technique required. There is no reason not to. There is no downside. The prospect doesn't know you and won't remember you called or asked two minutes after you hang up. Any obstacle is probably a lame attempt by your subconscious to defeat you. People generally want to help and they might if you ask. Prospects that need your help are out there. The person you are talking to might actually know one of them and be willing to point you in their direction.

BUILDING A REFERRAL-BASED BUSINESS

Nike has a long-running advertising slogan that can be very helpful in building a referral-based business – Just do it. You can ruminate about who and how to ask, and why you have trouble asking, and why others seem to get referrals and you don't, and what the underlying psychological reasons are. But in the end, you have to go out and ask.

So, to jump-start your referral flow -- Just do it. Ask for help. People who know you and respect you will help. Put your fears on the table and let your clients know you would like their help but it is OK if they can't for some reason.

Tell them you value your relationship and don't want this request to harm that relationship.

An example might be the following: "Ian, I am trying to expand my business and have found that my best new clients come as referrals from my best existing clients. I was wondering if you would be willing to help me. I don't want to put a strain on our relationship, so it is OK if you say, 'No.' I will understand."

The above is just a general example. Each request is different and depends upon the situation and the dynamics of the relationship.

GETTING TO "INTRODUCTION"

One of the best ways to overcome the reluctance of some clients to give you referrals is to have them provide introductions instead. In many cases, it may actually be easier to get an introduction than a referral.

But the first step to getting an introduction is to deal with their objection to giving you a referral. When your stockbroker or insurance agent asks you for a referral are you anxious to give them your friends' names? This can be a double-edged sword: Although you would like to help, you may be reluctant to provide the names of friends and colleagues to a trained killer salesperson who will pressure them into an appointment. After all, you don't want to risk your friends/colleagues' ire! So you respond by saying you can't think of anyone right now. But if you do you'll get back to them with any suggestions. (In other words, "No.")

The following illustrates how to turn a person who won't give you a referral into someone who will provide an introduction:

Salesperson: "I was wondering if you knew anyone you could refer me to."

Client: "I can't think of anyone right now."

Salesperson: "I know how you feel. I know that when someone asks me for a referral I am reluctant to give one because I am not sure how they will approach my friend or how my friend will react or even if she's willing to talk to them. I wouldn't want to put her in an awkward position."

Client: "That's exactly how I feel!"

Salesperson: "Then how about this? If you do know someone, you could call them and see if they were willing to talk to me. If they say 'Yes,' then you can give me their phone number. If the answer is "No," then no harm, no foul."

Client: "That's a great idea! I can think of a couple people I could call."

Salesperson: "Thanks! I'll follow up with you in a week or so."

The process is to get the client to give you the objection first. But the real secret is that you must have the right belief systems in place or no technique will be successful.

EMPOWER YOURSELF

Condition your own mindset. The best way to develop an empowering belief with regard to referrals is to give referrals yourself. That way, it will be hard for you to imagine why someone would not give one to you. Treat professional salespeople who cold call you with respect and try to help them out on occasion when you can. (It is not always possible to help and they are not all professional) If you act this way, you will come to expect that treatment, this expectation will communicate itself through your tonality and demeanor and you will begin to be treated accordingly.

18

Hidden Obstacles to Calling
at the Top

Fear is one of the most common emotions a new salesperson experiences. And calling at the top often brings up this emotion.

THE FEAR OF THE SECRET LANGUAGE

The most frequent reason for not calling at the top is fear of the supposedly secret language spoken in the executive suite. "Return on net assets" "Internal rate of return" -- What does it all mean? Feeling stupid is never pleasant and most people will go to great lengths to avoid that sensation. Salespeople immobilized by this fear imagine that executives are somehow different than everyone else. They ascribe many attributes to executives, not the least of which is the use of seemingly incomprehensible terminology and concepts. Because they do not know the "secret handshake," salespeople are afraid that they will not be taken seriously.

The Reality

Successful executives generally speak plainly. They rose to the top precisely because they have the ability to cut through obfuscation and see problems and situations in the most basic terms. Certain terms or phrases may come up from time to time that may not be in general use. However, there is no more variation in language going up the chain of command than from industry to industry.

Executives must be understandable because of the wide variety of people they communicate with. They need to get their point across to board members, public relations people, politicians, investors, civic groups, and employees at all levels. If on occasion they say something you do not understand, ask them to explain what they mean. It is no big deal and happens all of the time. In fact, you are more likely to say something they do not understand rather than the other way around.

THE FEAR OF LOOKING STUPID

Nightmares about looking stupid are common. Who hasn't had the dream about standing in front of their classmates saying or wearing the wrong thing, or perhaps nothing at all? A variation of this common fear is that the salesperson will say or do something inadvertently or unknowingly stupid in front of an important prospect. They are afraid their inadequate knowledge about protocol or lack of experience will cause them to look ignorant in front of executive prospects. In some cases, it is only fear of the unknown, which can be conquered through repetition. In others, no matter how many times they do it, they are uncomfortable at higher levels.

The Reality

You know your product or service better than anyone and that is what you are there to discuss. In many ways, things are actually easier at higher levels. Executives are busy but are also just like you -- regular people with a job to do. They do not have time to play games or to stand on protocol.

They agreed to see you because they had a problem they thought you could help with. Don't worry about saying the wrong thing because you should be mostly listening to their concerns. They will explain their problem, then you tell them about how your product or service will fix it. There is little chance of looking stupid in that scenario.

Of course, if you are using a sales process that does not meet the requirements set forth in chapter 8 you might have a problem. For instance, if you use a me-centered selling process and run through 50 PowerPoint slides detailing the product and how it works before even asking about the problem, you just might be shown the door prematurely. However, the Optimal Salesperson avoids me-centered selling. Instead he or she uses an effective selling system that focuses on the prospect, allowing for clear communication, eliminating any chance of looking stupid.

PROBLEMS WITH AUTHORITY FIGURES

Some people have a problem with authority figures and turn into a pile of mumbles in the presence of priests, rabbis, senators, pro athletes, and CEOs. Salespeople who suffer from this are easy to identify because they begin to act differently at the very thought of calling at the top. In some cases, you can see a physical reaction. As they begin to think about calling in the C-suite, they get nervous and start second-guessing what they should be saying. They see routine questions as intrusive and become unsure of themselves. They are afraid that whatever they say may be misinterpreted.

In transactional analysis terms, the sales call takes on the character of a parent-child interaction where the salesperson assumes the child role. When calling at lower levels in the organization, these same salespeople can carry on a normal adult-adult conversation.

Salespeople who assume a subservient role in the sales conversation will most certainly be less effective. Normal questions will be forgotten, verbal cues to ask probing questions will be ignored and they will be preoccupied with the fact that they are in the presence of "greatness." However, if you apply the principles of Chapter 10, you can overcome this problem rather easily.

The Reality

Authoritarian styles of management are passé. Inhabitants of the executive suite tend to be more collaborative and inclusive and employ a more participative management style. Yes, they have authority. Most, however, do not act like dictators. Even if they did, they have no authority over you (except, like any prospect, to say "Yes" or "No" to what you are selling).

As mentioned earlier in this chapter, executives are busy people and would not make time unless what you had to offer interested them. In this way, calling on an executive is easier than calling on someone lower in the organization. they don't waste time, they are decisive, and they don't have to check with as many people before moving ahead. As long as you go with the intent to quickly discover what the issue or problem is and discuss how you might be able to help, you should do just fine.

THE FEAR OF NOT BEING CREDIBLE

"Who am I to call on the CEO"? If you have this attitude, even subconsciously, you will feel major resistance to calling at the top. Rather than being in awe of the CEO, you feel you are not credible. That is, you do not know enough; you will not be believable; they will fail to take you seriously; and so on. You may tell yourself that it is your company or product you are worried about. Or you may feel it's not "right" to call on the CEO and instinctively call lower.

Sales managers will recognize this problem easily. When a salesperson is worried about their credibility in the executive suite, they will ask for help in making the call. They will offer to take the sales manager with them or request the assistance of their own CEO or of the chief technology officer.

The Reality

The executive knows nothing about you personally and frankly, is not interested. They only care about how you can solve their problem. Like you, they're someone with an important job to do and you may be able to help. If you are using a prospect-centered selling process as suggested in Chapter 8, your approach will most likely be to ask them questions to see if they have a problem that falls in your arena. Your credibility is established more by the questions you ask than any statements you make. It also helps to remember that in the vast majority of cases, the executive you are calling on knows little about your field of expertise. In fact, they will assume that you are the expert until you prove otherwise. And since you, the Optimal Salesperson, know your product or service area intimately, which questions to ask, and you focus on the prospect and the problem at hand, you may be the most credible salesperson they've ever met.

THE REALITY OF CALLING AT THE TOP

Sales Cycles Can Be Shorter

Most executives are decisive and make up their minds rapidly. That is the nature of their job. They generally have more latitude and authority to make decisions than people at the lower levels.

Major capital expenditures will usually have a procurement process that must be followed. However, you can quickly win the support of the executive in charge, even if the process takes much longer. Some executives will want to get buy-in from colleagues and even subordinates before they go ahead, but personal support from an executive gives you a leading edge. Starting at the top can significantly shorten the sales cycle because if the boss is interested in something, it becomes a higher priority for the lower levels. Issues will be addressed more quickly as your project moves to the "top of the stack."

Executives make the rules so it is sometimes easier for them to break them. If a project becomes important to the CEO, they can often figure a way around the rule or just plain ignore it. The rules are usually there to keep lower level managers in line with company policy. The executive knows the rationale for the rule and knows where to go to get dispensation from it if they do not have the authority themselves.

Executives got to where they are because they understand the organization. They know the company's "trip wires" and how to navigate the treacherous waters between where they are and where they want to be. It is exciting to watch an executive who "gets it" and wants your product or service, and bends the organization to meet his or her wishes. Your job is to understand their problem and show how you can help. Once you start calling at the top, you will wonder why you waited so long.

Problems Are Bigger

Ramifications of problems at the executive level are more far-reaching and have larger consequences. Therefore, executives tend to take a broader view and can either quickly see how your application can help or just as rapidly dismiss it as unworkable across the organization.

Many executives also have responsibility for multiple units so problems are naturally larger. Whether you are a consultant trying to improve efficiency or a copier salesperson selling document-imaging products, calling on executives will yield larger projects and reduce the amount of time it takes to reach your goals.

Case Study: Greg

Greg provided engineering services to a refinery. He worked with the local engineering office and was getting a fair amount of jobs but it was painful. Every project was price competitive and he had to fight tooth and nail to get projects approved by corporate management. His counterpart, the local project manager, could not make anything happen easily due to his lack of influence.

One day the work at the local refinery disappeared and Greg was outsold by a competitor. The competitor had called on the corporate vice-president responsible for all of the engineering work in the US based refineries and was subsequently awarded all of the work on a noncompetitive basis because she was able to show corporate management how to reduce overall cost by being more efficient. Greg learned his lesson and is now a believer in calling at the top.

Value, like beauty, is in the eye of the beholder. Executives are more able to perceive value, where others see only problems and cost, because they are trained to do so. For example, a local manager might view the "copier" in the office as part of the overhead. Selling to this manager might be difficult if the copier was doing an adequate job without too much down time. The local manager would see the purchase of the new copier as a cost. However, the executive vice-president responsible for 20 offices might see value in a document imaging system (composed of 20 copiers) which reduced paper usage across the company by a more efficient method of capturing and storing data for sharing between offices. Cost would be secondary to the value it would provide the company. Making a business case for the larger order might be easier than selling a single copier assuming that imaging, data storage, and data sharing have attracted the attention of the executive vice-president.

Fewer Obstacles

Obstacles that get in the way of smaller sales supported by lesser lights in the organization disappear in the face of bigger sales that solve larger problems championed by senior executives. The purchasing department is more cooperative. The project moves to the top of the priority list for staff members. Politics play less of a role. Delays are minimized and budgets materialize seemingly out of thin air. When the boss is behind something, others give in.

Anyone who's worked in business has witnessed this phenomenon. When upper management gets involved, it gets everyone's attention. Hardened positions soften and obstacles disintegrate, When the problem to be solved is big enough and the value to be gained large enough, that combination trumps whatever obstacle comes up.

THE BIG SECRET(S) ABOUT CALLING AT THE TOP

But here's the real secret: Executives can be as afraid of you as you are of them. This is especially true if you sell a technical product. Many executives are many years removed from dealing with the technical details of their businesses. They are concerned about not understanding your explanation of what you do and how your product or service works. Although this isn't always true, it is more often then you might think. Why else would they have people sit in on meetings with them?

It is exciting to discuss big problems with a person who has the stature and resources to be able to solve them. Calling at the top allows you to move projects more quickly and eliminate or avoid tedious obstacles to the sale. The paydays are larger and the company you keep is also more challenging and engaging.

The second secret about calling at the top is that it is so much fun it hardly seems like work at all. Whatever your fears are today about calling at the top, once you start doing it, you will likely discover them to be unfounded.

19

Hidden Obstacles to Closing

Closing is one of the more misunderstood facets of the sales process. Because there is so much pressure to close, it has many hidden obstacles. It takes the proper mindset to set the prospect up correctly so you can close easily.

CLOSING AND PRESSURE

The Self-Limiting Belief

The lack of a sales process causes salespeople to miss their time to close. They lack an understanding of when the prospect is ready to be closed so they resort to the ABC's of closing -- Always Be Closing. These salespeople believe that they should present the features and benefits of their product then begin to try "convincing" the prospect to buy with well-formed logic and well practiced "moves." This can come across to the prospect as arm-twisting and the sales interview can quickly degenerate into a confrontational encounter. Fortunately this sales method is rarely taught anymore. Nevertheless, the belief persists among salespeople and affects how they approach the task of closing a sale.

Salespeople with this perception of closing who are averse to confrontation and pressure will unconsciously avoid closing by not doing it at all. They talk, ask questions, present, and propose, but they never close and spend tremendous amounts of time in follow-up. Since they dislike pressure, they get few "No's" and have bloated pipelines.

The Reality

Prospects buy on their own timetable. The Optimal Salesperson makes sure they understand what the buyer's motivation is and their timetable for making a decision. He deftly guides the prospect through the process to the decision point. The close becomes the natural consequence of what went before and pressure is out of the equation.

Sales processes vary and closing techniques are sometimes a matter of personal preference, but if any sales process that meets the criteria outlined in Chapter 8 is used, then only a gentle nudge applied at the proper time may be required to close the sale. If you have to routinely resort to pressure to close or you avoid closing because you don't like to apply pressure, then you probably need to adjust your selling process.

AFRAID TO FAIL

The Self-Limiting Belief

When the prospect chooses not to do business with them, many salespeople see that as a failure. When the salesperson invests themselves emotionally in the pursuit, they tend to take a "No" especially hard, even personally. If a salesperson tries to avoid the disappointment associated with the loss of the opportunity to do business with a prospect, they will avoid trying to close. They think that if they do not close, they cannot hear the prospect say "No." If they have not said "No", there is still a chance that the answer could be a "Yes." They view the slim possibility of a "Yes" to be far better than a definite "No."

With this mindset, pipelines will balloon, time spent on proposals and follow-up calls will increase, prospecting time will decrease, and future sales will be in jeopardy. In addition, forecasting sales will be difficult and frustration will mount for both the salesperson and management as hoped-for sales never materialize.

The Reality

The word "No" does not equal failure in sales. Failure in sales is either not getting any decision at all or not reaching a sales goal. No one ever has 100 percent closing rate. Hearing the prospect tell you that they have decided to go with someone else is never pleasant. However, "No" is the second best word in sales (behind "Yes" of course!). It is far better than "We'll think it over," "Get back to us," or, "You are still being considered." "No" is part of the game of sales. If your closing rate is three out of ten, then you need the seven "No's" as much as you need the three "Yes's." Without the seven "No's" you have not been in front of ten people.

In addition, if your five-year average closing rate is thirty percent, then it is unlikely to suddenly rise to 100 percent overnight, if ever. The "No's" will be coming. So, when they do come, accept them as part of your job. Analyze what you did right and wrong and where you can improve the next time. An algebraic expression applies here: $(SW)^3$ which can be rewritten as SWSWSW which means Some Will; Some Won't; So What.

Getting the prospect to say "No" is good for another reason. Once the pursuit is over, you can stop wasting time on that opportunity and start finding the next one. With the proper mindset and an effective sales process, the pipeline will have no extraneous deals, wasted time will be minimized, frustration will diminish, and sales will increase.

The Optimal Salesperson thinks like an all-star major league baseball player. They know that they are paid for getting hits but that striking out is part of the game. Baseball players know that if they "fail" to get a hit seven out of ten times over a long enough period of time, they will be in the Hall of Fame at the end of their career. Optimal salespeople know that if they get enough "No's" over a long career in sales they will make more than enough money to meet their financial goals and have a great quality of life.

So adopt the mindset that, rather than being a failure "No" is just a success of a different type. That mindset will take most of the pressure off and help make you more effective and positive as you reach your sales goals.

FEAR OF REJECTION

The Self-Limiting Belief

Salespeople also have a deep fear of personal rejection. If it becomes too intense, it has many of the same effects as the fear of failure. Salespeople with this fear also avoid putting themselves in closing situations.

Rather than seeing the "No" as a failure on their part, the salesperson takes the "No" as a personal affront. The prospect says, "I do not want to buy your product" and the salesperson hears, "he hates me." When this happens, the salesperson is letting what was basically a business decision affect their self-concept. Take enough hits to your self-concept and you will start to think less of yourself and begin to feel oppressed. Oppression leads to depression which affects motivation. Many salespeople subconsciously protect their self-concept by avoiding closing situations as much as possible. Others stay out of sales altogether for this very reason.

The Reality

Personal attacks are rare in sales. In the vast majority of cases, the decision to buy from someone else is based on the product or service being delivered. It has nothing to do with you. Imagine a prospect saying, "I am going to buy this inferior product because I dislike (or want to stick it to) Charlie. Otherwise I'd purchase Charlie's product." Few if anyone would do such a thing.

Even when the service you are selling is one you will perform personally, the decision is rarely about you. Rather it's about the service itself. The prospect believes your competitor will perform the service better in some way, or that they can get the same result for less money or for some other reason. Admittedly, when selling a personal service this distinction is a little harder to make. It is easier if you realize they took exception to your approach or level of skill. It was not you as a person.

If for some strange reason, the prospect rejects you personally what exactly is there to fear? For a moment, imagine yourself rejected personally by the authors. Where does it hurt? How is your life different? You still have people who love you. Your dog will still be excited when you get home. We are not saying that you have to enjoy the rejection. However, put it in its proper perspective.

The Optimal Salesperson realizes that not every prospect buys his product or service and when this happens is not about them personally. If you adopt this mindset, you will put yourself in more closing situations and be better able to execute the sales techniques you know so well.

NEED FOR APPROVAL

The Self-Limiting Belief

As with fear of rejection and failure, need for approval will cause the salesperson to avoid closing situations and to be ineffective when they do try to close. (Chapter 11 has an extensive discussion of need for approval.) When salespeople seek approval from the prospects, they usually avoid asking tough questions because they do not want to lose their approval. So it's OK not to question why the prospect wants to put off the decision until next month even though they promised it for today. The salesperson will certainly shy away from reminding the prospect that a delay of a month means that the completion date, which seemed so important a few days ago, is now in jeopardy.

To salespeople with need for approval, it never seems like the proper time to close. Rather than avoiding failure or seeing it as personal affront, they try to win the prospect's approval by doing exactly what they are asked, whether it is the right thing or not. It is interesting that salespeople with this problem will risk losing the approval and respect of their family by jeopardizing their income and working long hours in an attempt win the approval of a prospect they may never see again. That behavior makes little sense, but need for approval is an emotional, visceral response rather than a logical decision.

Can you imagine the amount of internal conflict around closing for a salesperson with fear of failure, fear of rejection and need for approval? No wonder selling can be exhausting sometimes, which is why it's to your great benefit to conquer these hidden weaknesses.

The Reality

Replacing a need for approval with a need for respect is the best way to reframe and overcome this problem. You don't need approval from prospects –you can get it from friends, family, and colleagues. What you do need is to earn their respect by doing what's needed, when it is needed to be done.

Rather than involving pressure, closing requires recognizing the appropriate time for the prospect to make a decision and being willing to hear either a "Yes" or "No."

The Optimal Salesperson earns the approval of sales managers and family members and the respect of prospects by closing at the appropriate time. This is regardless of whether they get a "Yes" or a "No" and even if they do have to apply a little pressure.

THE DEAL IS BETTER IN MY PIPELINE THAN DEAD

The Self-limiting Belief

Large pipelines are valued by salespeople and provide them with a sense of comfort. They may not be closing anything this month but, "Things are looking up. I have a large pipeline!" It also looks good to management and to colleagues and keeps the salesperson busy. So busy in fact that they don't have time to prospect for new, more viable clients. This mindset will prevent the salesperson from moving prospects to a decision. If it's "No" (and there's a statistically good chance it might be) it has to come out of the pipeline. They would rather keep the deal on life support than end it.

The Empowering Mindset

Lose quickly if you are going to lose. The Optimal Salesperson thinks. "If I am ultimately going to lose, let me know today" and acts accordingly. During our seminars, when we ask participants when want to know if they are going to lose, 100 percent say, "Right now." But that is not how they act. They avoid closing and take put-offs and do whatever's necessary to keep the deals alive as long as possible.

The Optimal Salesperson knows that a large pipeline can provide a false sense of security. If the deals in the pipeline are low probability because the salesperson is administering sales CPR and postponing the inevitable, it will only result in wasted time in follow-up, reporting status to management, and embarrassment when forecasts are inaccurate.

The Optimal Salesperson closes at the right time, even if she or he has to ask tough questions. More importantly, if the prospect goes off track and it looks like the deal is going sour, the Optimal Salesperson seeks to halt the pursuit and find new prospects who are worth spending time with.

A NON-SUPPORTIVE PERSONAL BUY CYCLE

As a Weakness

Chapter 14 discussed how personal buying habits can make an impact on sales effectiveness. One particular part of the buy cycle has a major effect on closing - decisiveness. If a salesperson is indecisive when making a major purchase, she will be vulnerable in situations where the prospects can't make up their minds and want to put off the decision. The salesperson will have empathy for the plight of the prospects and allow them to "sleep on it" or to "think about it" for a few days. When the prospect has promised a decision and, when it's time to close the deal, gives either of those excuses, the salesperson with the same weakness caves in every time. This is a difficult problem to diagnose because the fact that the deal needs to be closed may never come to this salesperson's mind.

As a Strength

Buying everything is not the answer. The Optimal Salesperson recognizes when it is time to make a buying decision and makes it without undue hesitation or over analysis. They decide what they need, why they need it, how much they are willing to pay, and then go to a place they trust and buy it. (Assuming, of course, that the store has what is needed at the price they are willing to pay). A salesperson who operates this way will be better able to identify the correct time to close. However, more importantly, when the time to close comes, they will close and not be put off. This means they get either a "Yes" or a "No" and move on from there.

A salesperson with a supportive buy cycle will be much more successful at getting decisions from their prospects.

It will make no sense why the decision cannot be made now since that is what the prospect promised and nothing has changed. Thus, they will execute their sales process and either win the deal or lose, but they will get a decision.

If you are having trouble with closing, take note of your own personal buying habits. You may be poisoning your mindset with customer empathy.

IT IS OK IF THEY SHOP AROUND

The Self-Limiting Belief

Comparison shopping is the bane of the closer. If you believe that it is OK to shop around then you will find yourself plagued by shoppers in your pipeline. It's important to differentiate between prospects and shoppers – the former are looking for a particular product or service, while the latter are solely interested in price. They will be shopping and you will be chasing them. Contributing to this problem is the belief that "the product sells itself." It is admirable to believe in the superiority of your product, but no product possesses closing skills.

Salespeople with these attitudes will default to a me-centered selling approach -- when a shopper is interested, they begin the show and tell, with little regard to specific needs. After all, they reason, the shopper should have all of the data if they are going to compare; especially the data that gives their product an advantage. Salespeople with this attitude will fail to ask questions and refuse to probe deeply for underlying buying motives. However, they will provide data, ideas, specifications, and price proposals to prospects who are really shoppers. In most cases the shopper gathers the data and moves onto the next vendor, using your information to get a better deal.

The Empowering Mindset

The Optimal Salesperson believes that people who are shopping are ultimately buying based on price, and since she does not always have the cheapest price, the price shopper will rarely buy from her. The Optimal Salesperson does not just dismiss the shopper, but her empowering mindset causes her to act in a totally different and more effective fashion.

Realizing that the shopper is less than ideal, the Optimal Salesperson does not worry about hearing a "No." They don't give out free ideas and won't write quotes until the prospect has been converted to a value buyer and meets their qualification criteria according to their sales process. They ask probing questions, discover early that price is the determining factor, and advise the prospect that they don't usually have the lowest price. Ultimately, they either qualify the prospect to be in their pipeline or end up spending little time on them. Optimal Salespeople never provide the prospect with leverage they can use to get better deal from someone else.

You may be tempted to ask, "OK, so what are the magic techniques to make that happen?" But it's not the techniques that enable you to eliminate prospects from shopping you. It is adopting the right belief. Once you believe it is <u>not</u> OK to shop around and stop doing it yourself, whatever words you use will work just fine.

20

The Hidden Walls of Your Comfort Zone

Expectation might be the best way to describe a <u>comfort zone</u>. Everyone has expectations. You have expectations about what someone with your skills should earn. You have an expectation of what you deserve. Strange as it may seem, sometimes that expectation is lower than what you are currently being paid. When you make sales calls, you expect to get certain results. If the results vary from what you expect, you adjust until there is a match.

Comfort zone applies to every aspect of sales, from who you call on to your closing rate. It will include the questions you ask and the answers you accept. <u>Growth</u> is the process of breaking through the walls of your current comfort zone and establishing a new comfort zone at a higher level of functioning.

WHAT DEFINES YOUR COMFORT ZONE?

<u>Self-image</u> is how you see yourself in relation to the world

and can relate to many aspects of your life. In this context it refers to how you see yourself relative to other salespeople, prospects, and your general socioeconomic status. If a salesperson sees herself as a top level, high performing salesperson then she will expect her financial results to be among the best in the office or in the industry she works in. If results don't match how she sees herself, then she will adjust her approach or her effort until they do. Likewise, if a salesperson sees herself as middle-of the road, that's how she will perform.

The Optimal Salesperson views himself as a professional whose normal sphere of operation is at higher levels of the organization. He feels comfortable there because he "belongs." An underperforming salesperson will see himself as a vendor who should call on purchasing agents and does not belong in the executive suite. A top-earning salesperson can live where he wants and feels good when he can afford to live in an expensive neighborhood. Comfort zone is hindering growth when the salesperson cannot see himself living in those neighborhoods or feels second class around people who do. The Optimal Salesperson can choose to live anywhere but would fit in with the people whether they reside in a mansion or a one-bedroom apartment. It's not where you actually live or what you own that matters; it is how you see yourself that makes the difference

Confidence is related to but slightly different from self-image. Confidence defines the comfort zone because the more confident you are in an arena, the more likely you will perform well in that arena. Confidence is a function of ability and experience. The cycle of confidence is depicted in Figure 21.1 on page 231.

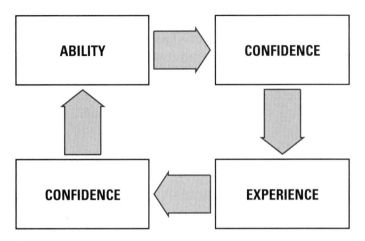

Figure 21.1. Cycle of Confidence

If a salesperson knows he has the ability to perform well, he will have confidence. A confident salesperson will gain experience with both positive and negative results. Experience will lead to more confidence and more confidence coupled with more experience will lead to more ability. Confidence bolstered by ability and experience will make the salesperson more comfortable at higher levels of performance.

<u>History</u> has a profound effect on a salesperson's comfort zone. History means the total of all things you have been exposed to in your life up to this point. If one of your parents is the CEO of a $100 million company, the chances are that you grew up around corporate executives. Your parents' friends were presidents and vice-presidents and your friends' parents held similar positions. As a salesperson, you would feel very comfortable in the presence of executives since you had been around them all of your life. However, if your parents were waiters or laborers you might feel uneasy in that arena at first. It would take some effort on your part to get comfortable in the executive suite.

Your history is also the total of all of your experiences, both positive and negative. If your first foray into the executive suite was traumatic or upsetting, you would likely not to want to repeat the experience. If you try a new technique or sales process that is wildly successful the first time, you'll probably want to do it again and again, feeling more comfortable with it each time.

Society helps define a salesperson's comfort zone. When a person grows up in a certain neighborhood, certain expectations can be ingrained. These expectations will help define the initial possibilities the person will see for themselves. How much money you can earn or deserve, who you should associate with, and what you should do for a living are all affected by the society you grow up in. Of course, parental input will have an equally profound effect. The effect of society and parental input can be either positive or negative. They can define a comfort zone of high or low functioning. However, as encouraging or discouraging this initial comfort zone may be, it is not a life sentence. It is just a starting point. The world is full of examples of people who rose above their circumstances to achieve greatness and an equal number who were born to privilege and accomplished nothing.

Self-limiting beliefs also play a major role in determining the walls of the comfort zone. Many beliefs are a function of society, parenting, and experiences as described above. But you acquire other beliefs from co-workers, managers, or friends. These beliefs set your expectations which help define your comfort zone. For example, if a salesperson somehow comes to believe that getting referrals in his particular industry is difficult, he will expect to be rejected if he asks for them. With the expectation of failure and possibly coupled with a need for approval, the salesperson will be uncomfortable asking for referrals. The fact that asking for referrals is outside his comfort zone will limit his effectiveness since he will have to spend more time cold calling to fill the pipeline.

As salespeople systematically eliminate self-limiting beliefs, their comfort zone will expand. They will become increasingly at ease when calling at higher levels and will use more effective selling processes and techniques and earn more money. The Optimal Salesperson is in a continual process of identifying the walls of his or her comfort zone and moving them higher.

WHY ARE YOU STUCK?

The unknown is a great source of fear; and <u>fear of the unknown</u> is one of the primary emotions that keep us stuck in our comfort zone. You may find this especially true when trying to get salespeople to adopt a new sales process or technique. Sometimes they would rather fail fifty times in a row using a familiar technique than try something that is a "stretch." When asked why, the answer invariably has something to do with how they will feel or will be perceived using the new technique. Sometimes this has to do with need for approval, but more often it is a comfort zone issue.

When growth starts to become significant, another type of fear can set in and keep you locked in your comfort zone. That is the <u>fear of change</u>, of being a different person than you are right now. People resist change sometimes, even when it's for the better. The psychology behind this phenomenon is beyond the scope of this book. Just realize that if you feel resistance to growth, fear of change may be the problem. A closely related issue is the <u>fear of success</u>. It seems strange, but many people are afraid of success. They may not admit it openly but their actions tell the story. This is basically a combination of the fear of the unknown and not wanting to change into a different person.

Guilt is an emotion that can keep you from growing at the rate you would like. It can manifest itself in many ways, both big and small. If you were told as a child not to interrupt when "grown-ups" are busy, then you may feel guilty making cold calls because the prospects may be busy. A salesperson may also feel guilty for earning a lot of money. They feel like they don't deserve it or that it is unfair that they make so much when others have so much less. Once you become conscious of these guilty feelings, they are relatively easy to overcome.

However, guilt most often operates more on the subconscious level. It takes introspection to realize that guilt might be holding you in your comfort zone. If you feel resistant to growth or if it is slow in coming, consider that you might be dealing with guilt. Listen to your self-talk as you set goals and make plans. You may hear a familiar voice saying, "Who are you kidding? You can't have that. Who do you think you are? Why should you have those things when your brother works just as hard and is just getting by?"

A feeling of inevitability also prevents growth and keeps us stuck in our comfort zone. If you feel the die is cast and there is nothing you can do to get out of your current situation, you will be discouraged. Discouragement leads to inaction. You will give up mentally and you will be defeated before you even begin. A case in point is the apocryphal story of how elephants are trained. Supposedly one of the elephant's hind legs is tied to a stake in the ground with a heavy chain. The elephant strains at the tether trying to get away but soon learns that he cannot pull the stake from the ground or break the chain. Soon the elephant learns he is stuck and stops trying to get away.

After awhile the elephant trainers replace the chain with a thick rope. From time to time the elephant gives it a halfhearted yank. But without a real effort, the elephant remains unsuccessful in his escape attempts. The handlers replace the thick rope with a thinner one and the elephant remains tethered because by this time he has given up. Discouragement has relegated the elephant to a life tethered by bonds he could easily break if he put his mind to it and really tried. He is a prisoner of his own making.

HOW DOES THE COMFORT ZONE WORK?

Any activity with an outcome of "success" or "failure," can illustrate how concept of comfort zone works. For instance, Michael is a fairly good neighborhood basketball player. He expects to make half of the shots from 15-18 feet of the basket; that is his comfort zone. If Michael goes out one day and hits his first shot, he is not surprised; he had a 50 percent chance of hitting that shot. If he then proceeds to hit the next and the next and then the next two or three, at some point he starts to think, "Hey, I am hot today." Then say, after six shots are made, he misses. One of the first things that goes through his mind is, "Well, I knew that had to happen. I couldn't keep up that pace." He will then proceed to miss enough to get back to his average of 50 percent.

Michael had a string of successes <u>outside</u> of his comfort zone. He noticed and as soon as he became aware of what he was doing, unconsciously corrected his actions to revert to "normal" behavior. Now if instead of a backyard player, suppose Michael was the NBA shooting champion. He would not even notice that he had hit six 15-foot shots in a row. It is not unusual for him to hit 19 out of 20 23-foot shots in practice. His comfort zone is much higher. In fact, if he missed after only six shots made he might think, "What's wrong? That's not supposed to happen."

However, if Michael, the neighborhood player, missed the first six shots he would think, "I am not a great shooter, but I am not this bad." He would concentrate more and pay attention to his form until the shots started to fall into the basket. In other words, he adjusted until he got back to where he thought he belonged ... at a 50 percent success rate.

That is how the comfort zone works. When you get outside it, you will somehow work to get yourself back to the success rate you are comfortable with. Most salespeople, though they say they believe in the concept of a comfort zone, rebel at the idea that they are somehow responsible for their own failure. However, if you want to dramatically increase your income or your effectiveness and sustain it, you must work to move the comfort zone upwards. That will require lots of effort on your part.

Lottery winners who go from minimum wage to big bucks provide another example. One study showed that within three years of winning the lottery, most winners were in worse financial shape than ever and would have in fact been better off not winning.

The reason has to do with their comfort zone. Lottery winners are instantly catapulted into a new arena for which they are typically unprepared. Everything is different. Before their big win, they knew how to parcel out their paycheck. Now they have no idea how to handle hundreds of thousands of dollars. They are uncomfortable in their new, fancy neighborhood. They fall prey to scams due to their lack of financial knowledge and are unprepared for the decisions that come with managing large sums of money.

Many winners longed to return to simpler days when their friends weren't jealous and people liked them for who they were, not what they had. Those who fail to acknowledge this openly often subconsciously practice self-sabotage so that they can get back to where they are comfortable.

BREAKING THROUGH THE WALLS OF THE COMFORT ZONE

People avoid doing what they are afraid of. It has been our observation that what salespeople are afraid will happen on sales calls doesn't ever happen. They are afraid people will hang up on them. They are afraid prospects will throw them out of their office. They are afraid prospects will be upset when asked certain questions. The result is that they don't ask tough questions and they don't prospect; or if they do, it is in a weak-kneed manner and they don't get the result they feared but they also don't get the results they were hoping for. Of course they don't find many projects to put in their pipeline either.

Having strategized literally thousands of sales calls, we can tell you that 95 percent of the time what the salesperson is most afraid of almost never happens. Other things do occur, but usually not what the salesperson worried about.

With this in mind think of the word "fear" as the acronym F.E.A.R. = False Expectations Appearing Real. As discussed in earlier chapters, there is nothing to fear in sales. No physical harm can come to you. Rejection is not painful especially when you realize that is not you they are rejecting. Fear is just the body's way of getting us ready to perform at your best. Fear gets the "juices flowing" and heightens your senses so that you can be at your best in front of the prospect.

The most effective way to handle the fear about performing an activity in sales is to feel the fear, recognize that nothing really bad can happen, and "do it" anyway. Do what you fear the most and it will become your greatest ally. Once you conquer the fear by acting in the face of it, that action will become routine. You will ask tough questions, be better at qualifying, and so on. Your work will rise to a new level. Your competition will most likely still be the same level, and you will have a competitive advantage. Do this over and over again and you will be at the top of the heap.

Guilt is another emotion that can hold you in your comfort zone. Many guilty feelings have their origins in admonitions parents give to children to keep them safe or to teach valuable lessons. Rules such as, "Don't speak to strangers," "Don't interrupt when adults are talking," and "Don't speak unless spoken to" were designed to keep you out of trouble and develop social graces. They might have been good advice for a seven-year-old but can get in the way of being a successful salesperson.

"Don't ask for too much" and "Money is the root of all evil" are other axioms that help a young person develop priorities in life, but may be getting in the way of achieving sales quotas now. Discovering the source of your internal resistance is the arena of a therapist. However, therapy is hardly necessary to be successful in sales.

Just realize that your "gut" feelings are based on rules set up long ago for a situation that no longer exists. You are in a new situation now with new rules. What was forbidden in the past is required today. Fight through the feeling and do what you know must be done, and you will establish a new comfort zone. It doesn't mean you have changed as a person. You are the same person operating under different, more appropriate standards of behavior.

Wallowing in a feeling of <u>discouragement</u> will perpetuate the results you are feeling badly about. Unsuccessful salespeople act how they feel. When they feel down, they do little, if anything to improve their lot. Inaction leads to stagnation and prolongs the cycle of failure. The Optimal Salesperson realizes that how you act determines how you feel, not the other way around.

Therefore, even though from time they may feel somewhat discouraged, they continue to act. Action yields results. Attitudes change, discouragement disappears, and is replaced by optimism. Optimism yields still more actions and a new cycle of success begins. The comfort zone is expanded and new victories await.

Don't let discouragement hold you down. Sales is a profession where you are not in total control and sometimes things don't go your way despite doing everything right. However, if you keep moving forward, good things will happen.

21

Conclusion: Putting It All Together to Achieve Exponential Growth

By now you should have a good understanding of what makes up the Optimal Salesperson. It all fits together in a certain order. First, it's important to understand that sales is more than a job. Then you need to get and stay motivated, institute goals management and prospecting programs and then adopt and adapt an effective sales process. Next you need to commit to personal growth and begin to identify and eliminate the hidden weaknesses that are holding you back.

SALES IS NOT A JOB

Job holders typically trade hours for dollars. And, in most jobs such as physical labor, accounting, engineering, administration, and even senior management, the secret to success is to work harder and do more. Such is not the case with sales. The "hard" work of sales is overcoming the hidden weaknesses that hold you back.

In sales, sometimes less is more. Getting strong enough to ask better questions will allow the Optimal Salesperson to eliminate work. For example, if you can get the prospect to tell you what they want to spend, it takes less time and emotional energy to develop a quote. If you get better at qualifying prospects you will write fewer quotes to win the same amount of business, allowing you more time to find bigger and better prospects. The clock is not very relevant when measuring the efforts of salespeople. Spending more time asking the same old questions and getting the same answers will stall success in sales.

A salesperson's compensation can seem disproportionate to the effort expended. At the beginning of their career, they are typically underpaid. After years of hard work and growth, and having overcome the majority of the hidden weaknesses, they can command what seems to be a kings' ransom to an hourly worker. So avoid approaching sales as a "regular job," trading and measuring your hours against the company's dollars. Treat it as if you were an entrepreneur, investing your effort and emotional energy in the beginning for large rewards in the end.

MOTIVATE YOURSELF

Impotent goals lead to lack of motivation and stagnated growth. Who gets motivated just to get out of debt? How thrilled will you be next year if you are one percent better than you were this year and can therefore afford three percent less stuff due to inflation? Develop and write down compelling personal goals. Get your spouse involved. Give yourself a reason to expend the energy it will take to grow. See Chapter 4 for details on how to accomplish this.

Maintaining your desire for success amid the daily battles with prospects and your own hidden weaknesses can be difficult. When you are up to your butt in alligators sometimes it is hard to remember that your original purpose was to drain the swamp. Determination to succeed is essential to growth. Without it, the smallest obstacles will spell stagnation and defeat. Review your goals daily to maintain your desire for success at the highest level. Keeping your goals in sight at all times will ensure that you will endure short-term pain for long-term gain.

STAY MOTIVATED

Protecting your outlook is an essential part of staying motivated. If you begin to believe that the market is tough and times are bad, you can start to wonder why you are bothering to put in the effort since, "It won't make any difference, people just aren't buying." Chapter 5 describes how outlook is a force multiplier on your efforts. Naysayers are everywhere. Be careful what ideas you let into your head. Healthy people limit their intake of fat and grease. Similarly, strong salespeople limit the amount and type of negative ideas that they allow into their thoughts. Reality, no matter how seemingly deleterious it is to your business, always has a bright side. Concentrate on the "glass half-full" and your outlook will remain optimistic and your motivation strong.

Adjust to changes. The world is a constantly changing place; the Optimal Salesperson is able to adapt. The first step should be to take responsibility and refuse to play the victim. Lost sales should be simply viewed as outcomes of conditions and actions taken, rather than failures. With this approach, your belief systems remain strong as you adjust your approach and get a different and most likely better result. Doing and adapting will also go a long way toward maintaining a high level of motivation.

INSTITUTE AND MAINTAIN A GOALS MANAGEMENT PROGRAM

Consistent sales activity is essential to growth. Once you know your destination (goals) and are sufficiently motivated, and have determined the level of sales activity needed to reach your goals, then track your sales activity on a daily basis and review it regularly to ensure that you are on course. Also, be reasonable when setting activity goals.

You need to be consistent when tracking activity as well as reviewing and adjusting the activity based on actual results. Results will vary over time as your skills improve and the conditions in the marketplace change. Chapter 6 goes into more detail on how to develop and maintain a sales activity plan that will help you manage your progress in achieving goals.

GET A PROSPECTING PROGRAM

A consistent flow of prospects is the lifeblood of the Optimal Salesperson. You must have a process for generating enough of the right kind of prospects to meet your goals. Depending on your type of business, the stage of your career, and the goals you have set, you will use some combination of cold calls, referrals, and introductions to generate prospects. The Optimal Salesperson tends to focus more on introductions and Chapter 7 explains how to develop a network of introduction sources to keep your pipeline full. Make sure you have a clear understanding of where prospects are coming from and the type and amount of activity needed to get them into your pipeline at the appropriate rate.

ADOPT A SELLING PROCESS AND HONE YOUR INTERPERSONAL SKILLS

Sales processes are a dime a dozen. Hundreds of books and tens of thousands of hours of sales training have been devoted to them. Yet when we evaluate salespeople and sales teams, we rarely find any evidence of consistent use of any sales process. Ones that are implemented are usually quite ineffective leading to wasted time, low close rates, and frustrated business owners.

Choose an effective sales process appropriate to your industry; adapt it to your particular situation; and use it consistently. Chapter 8 describes the attributes of an effective sales process. We recommend the baseline selling model developed by Dave Kurlan (BASELINE SELLING, Author House, 2005); it meets all of the criteria and can be adapted to fit most if not all selling situations.

Practice, practice, and more practice is required to hone your selling skills so that you react automatically and appropriately to what the prospect says and does. Professional athletes practice daily so they can instinctively perform their skill on the field without having to think through every action. The Optimal Salesperson should do the same. Prepare for calls so you know the approach to take. Rely on your skills to carry you through the call as you focus on the prospect. And debrief yourself and make adjustments for your next call. This process of preparation, execution, feedback, and adjustment will eventually allow you to develop the skill level to handle any selling situation and get your desired outcome.

COMMIT YOURSELF

Make success mandatory. Leave yourself no options. Raise your expectation of yourself and do not make excuses for not doing what needs to be done. In short, commit. Commit yourself to the level of sales activity; commit yourself to getting out of your comfort zone and using the sales process you have adopted; commit yourself to the effort it will take to overcome your hidden weaknesses. If you have trouble holding yourself responsible, get someone you respect to act as an accountability partner. A sales coach who understands the interrelationships of the attributes of the Optimal Salesperson can accelerate your growth curve. But don't wait for the right time or mentor. Employ Nike's motto and "Just do it."

OVERCOME YOUR HIDDEN WEAKNESSES

Identifying which hidden weakness to work on is very important. You cannot overcome them all simultaneously or instantaneously. The best thing to do is target the self-limiting belief or hidden weakness that is having the largest effect on you and your sales. For example, if you are constantly dealing with price issues, you may want to start by working on money weakness. Work on one or two weaknesses at a time but do so consistently. You will know when to begin work on a new weakness when a different issue shows up consistently as an obstacle to your success or you suddenly realize that your original belief has changed. Parts IV and V of this book are devoted to identifying and overcoming your hidden obstacles to success.

THE CYCLE OF GROWTH

Growth is rarely uniform. The effort should be consistent, however. Everyone is aware that children go through growth spurts. They eat regularly but growth sometimes comes in short, concentrated bursts. So it is with personal development when becoming an Optimal Salesperson. Effort should be regular and consistent (like eating) but the growth will come in spurts. The cycle becomes -- set goals, force sales activity, practice new sales skills as you use your new sales process. Hidden weaknesses will present themselves. Work on those and then one day you will look around and notice that you have grown significantly. It might not be obvious when it happens. Then you do it all over again. Revise the goals, set the activity level, on and on for the rest of your very successful sales career.

It will be hard work, but it will be rewarding. And remember that success is not a destination but a journey. With effort and determination, you can become the Optimal Salesperson you were meant to be.

DOES YOUR SALES TEAM HAVE WHAT IT TAKES TO GROW YOUR COMPANY

We help companies grow by:

Working With Your Existing Sales Force

- How far are they form being the Optimal Salesperson
- Can they ever become the optimal sales person
- Is Sales Management doing all it can do to grow your company
- Do you have the systems and processes in place for growth

Recruiting Sales Professionals for You

- We find, qualify, interview, and test candidates before you see them.
- You hire only Optimal Sales people

Assisting Your own Recruiting Efforts

- Pre-test to determine hidden weaknesses
- Train you on how to identify and hire The optimal salesperson

CARAMANICO MAGUIRE ASSOCIATES, INC.

SALES FORCE DEVELOPMENT EXPERTS

Visit **www.caramanico.com** for a free sales force grader or a free sales achievement grader or call 610-940-4430